BEIJING

THE BIOGRAPHY OF A CITY

JONATHAN CLEMENTS

SUTTON PUBLISHING

First published in the United Kingdom in 2008 by
Sutton Publishing, an imprint of NPI Media Group Limited
Cirencester Road · Chalford · Stroud · Gloucestershire · GL6 8PE

British Library Cataloguing in Publication Data
A catalogue record for this book is available from the British
Library.

ISBN 978-0-7509-4251-5

Photographs by Kati Clements
© Muramasa Industries Limited, 2006.

Typeset in Melior.
Typesetting and origination by
NPI Media Group Limited.
Printed and bound in England.

For
Lily Block

welcome to my world

Also by Jonathan Clements

Wu: The Chinese Empress Who Schemed, Seduced and Murdered Her Way to Become a Living God

The First Emperor of China

Confucius: A Biography

Pirate King: Coxinga and the Fall of the Ming Dynasty (published in paperback as *Coxinga and the Fall of the Ming Dynasty*)

Mao

Marco Polo

The Moon in the Pines

A Brief History of the Vikings

The Dorama Encyclopedia: A Guide to Japanese Television Drama Since 1953 (with Motoko Tamamuro)

The Anime Encyclopedia: A Guide to Japanese Animation Since 1917 (with Helen McCarthy)

The Little Book of Chinese Proverbs

Contents

Map by Martin Stiff

Chronology

294	Local inhabitants, even foreign immigrants, pool their resources and labour to repair flood and earthquake damages in the region.
c. **300**	The city is renamed *Youzhou* – the Tranquil City.
314	The region falls under the influence of non-Chinese races, including the Xianbei and Toba – both regarded by the Chinese as 'barbarian' races.
337–70	State of Former Yan
384–409	State of Later Yan
384–94	Western Yan
398–410	Southern Yan
409–35	Northern Yan
607	The region is linked by a canal with the south, brought back within the orbit of 'Chinese' rulers.
611	Youzhou is a staging post for armies of the new Sui dynasty for attacks on Korea.
644	The Taizong Emperor of the Tang dynasty returns to Youzhou in an attempt to complete his predecessors' military actions.
645	Taizong builds the Temple of the Origin of the Law, a cenotaph in memory of Chinese soldiers fallen in Korea.
755	The city is a major base in the rebellion of An Lushan against the Tang dynasty.
759	A local attempts to proclaim a Yan 'dynasty', but fails.
917	Early incursions of Khitan tribesmen. The region is largely depopulated as Chinese colonists flee south for their own safety. Slow commencement of three centuries of North–South division.

1025	Only a couple of generations after their arrival, the Khitan rulers have been sufficiently sinicised to want to imitate the Chinese in the south. Examinations and sacrifices in Yanjing follow Chinese traditional models.
1115	The Jurchen tribesmen of the hinterland proclaim a new 'Chinese' dynasty, the Jin or 'Golden'.
1120	The emperor of the Song dynasty unwisely attempts to oust the Khitans by arranging a deal with the Khitans' Jurchen rivals. Instead of restoring the region to the Song, the Jurchen take it for themselves. The city becomes Zhongdu, the 'Middle Capital' of the Jin.
1192	Completion of the 'Marco Polo' Bridge.
1211	First Mongol attack on Zhongdu.
1215	Fall of Zhongdu to the Mongols.
1266	Khubilai Khan orders the reconstruction of Zhongdu. Extensive remodelling of the water system. The city is renamed *Dadu* or *Taidu*, the Great City.
1275	Arrival of Marco Polo in China. He writes of Dadu as *Cambaluc*, thought to be his transliteration of the Turkish Khanbalikh – 'the Khan's City.'
1293	Completion of the new canal link to the south.
1345	Famines and floods lead to anti-Mongol unrest.
1368	Mongols driven out of China by the new Chinese Ming dynasty. The cityis renamed Beiping – 'Northern Peace'.

1371   Extensive reconstruction in Beiping, as the administrative centre of the emperor's fourth son.

1402   The fourth son of the late emperor seizes the throne, proclaiming himself to be Yongle, the Emperor of Perpetual Happiness. He relocates the capital to his own power base, and Beiping is renamed Beijing – Northern Capital – for the first time.

1530   Construction of the altars to the Sun, Moon and Earth.

1601   Arrival of Matteo Ricci, a Jesuit missionary, in Beijing.

1644   Beijing is captured by the armies of the Manchus. The last Ming emperor hangs himself from a tree on Coal Hill, north of the Forbidden City.

1648   All Chinese residents are banished from the inner city of Beijing, which becomes a sector reserved exclusively for Manchus.

1694   Russian community in Beijing begins to grow.

1745   Early work begins on the gardens of the Summer Palace.

1793   Visit by the first British ambassador to China, George Macartney.

1831   Flooding near the Marco Polo Bridge.

1896   Completion of the first railway between Beijing and Tianjin.

1900   The Boxer uprising and the subsequent occupation of the city by foreign troops.

1902   Cixi, the Empress Dowager, returns to Beijing by train.

1912   Abdication of the Last Emperor.

1916	Yuan Shikai fails in his bid to become the first emperor of a new dynasty, and dies later the same year.
1919	Events at the Paris Peace Conference lead to the 4 May demonstrations in Beijing.
1920	First Chinese Communist organisation founded in Beijing.
1928	Nanjing is the capital again. Beijing renamed Beiping.
1937	The Marco Polo Bridge incident sees the first shots fired in the Second Sino-Japanese War.
1938	Japanese occupy Beiping and rename it Beijing once more.
1941	Japanese attack on Pearl Harbor. US and British residences in Beijing are occupied by the Japanese military.
1945	At the close of the Second World War, Beijing is contested between Chinese Nationalist and Communist forces.
1948	Communist forces surround Beijing.
1949	Surrender of Nationalists in Beijing. Chairman Mao proclaims the foundation of a new Communist state – the People's Republic of China.
1959	The tenth anniversary of the PRC sees central Beijing remodelled with Soviet-style architecture and a wide open space in front of the Tiananmen gate.
1968	The army is deployed in Beijing in order to quell fighting between rival factions of Red Guards.
1971	Construction begins on the Beijing subway.
1972	Richard Nixon visits China.

1976	Death of Chairman Mao. His mausoleum is built in Tiananmen Square.
1985	Rioting in Beijing after the home team loses a soccer match against Hong Kong.
1986	Queen Elizabeth II visits China.
1989	Student demonstrations in Tiananmen Square are suppressed with tanks.
1990	Beijing hosts the Asian Games.
1993	Failed bid to hold the 2000 Olympics.
2001	Beijing's bid to host the 2008 Olympics is successful.

Introduction

There are many guides to Beijing and all tell the same story. Chinese tradition rarely recognises an inherent value in a mere building – houses and palaces are often nothing but bricks, beams and tiles, liable to burn or fall down, and easily replaced. It is a location itself, its natural features and history, that endures. In 1935, L.C. Arlington and William Lewisohn lamented the difficulties of writing an accurate guidebook to Beijing, and the possibility that readers might become irritated when they were unable to find monuments or buildings about which they had read:

> This, unfortunately, is not the fault of the authors – they would be only too glad if it was – but is due to the indifference of the Chinese themselves, more especially of their authorities, towards the historical monuments in which Peking is so rich. The loss by vandalism and utter neglect has been proceeding at such a rate that, on repeated occasions, buildings and historical monuments have actually disappeared while the authors are still writing about them.[1]

Their complaint is a common one, repeated throughout history. Singers of the Dark Ages lamented the overgrown ruins of what had been the capital of the Land of Swallows. Retreating Mongols bemoaned the fate of their once-great Khan's City, doomed, or so they thought, to fall into disrepair. In 2006, as I walked the dingy, grey paths of a 1950s slum, my guide announced sorrowfully that this, too, would soon pass, demolished to make way for Olympic hotels. Perhaps, hundreds of thousands of years ago, Peking Man looked over the rubble from his fallen cave roof, shook his head and grunted that the place was falling apart.

When Arlington and Lewisohn wrote, they were scathing about the removal of priceless treasures to the south. What would they have said if they had known what we know now, that those same treasures were not 'doomed to be eaten by moths, or destroyed by the damp'? Instead, they were spirited away to Taiwan, where they remain, regarded by some as an act of outrageous theft, and by others as an act of fortuitous mercy. Had the retreating Republicans not taken the treasures with them, they might have been destroyed forever during the chaos of Mao's Cultural Revolution.

The early Communist era saw much of the old city demolished to make way for modernisation. Palaces were turned into dormitories; the city walls were pulled down to make space for a ring road. Tiananmen Square, that internationally infamous void at China's heart, is a relatively recent part of the city's mythos – the product of town-planning one-upmanship during the Cold

War, when Mao was determined to have a parade ground to beat Red Square in Moscow.

This is not an exacting tourist guide to Beijing; it is a biography of a living subject. From my own experience, travel manuals date all the faster in an Olympic city. I will not be telling you the bus fare to a street that will soon disappear, nor will I be telling you which of six boarded-up buildings served me the best Chinese food some years ago. This book will tell you Beijing's story – how the city has looked to thousands of generations of its inhabitants, its legends and its tales of rags to riches, to rags again and riches once more.

Despite its modern incarnation as the quintessence of China, Beijing sits at the crossroads of cultures. For many centuries of its history, it has not been a wholly 'Chinese' city at all, since some of its most influential denizens have been from cultures to which Chinese histories disparagingly refer to as 'barbarian'. Many such barbarians have soon been assimilated; some, like the Mongols and the Manchus, are indistinguishable to the average Westerner from the Chinese themselves. Such reversals of fortune have led to multiple name-changes over the years – Beijing has been the South Capital, Tranquil City, Northern Peace, the Middle City, the Great Metropolis, the Place of Thistles and the Bitter Sea. In an effort to keep things simple, I refer to it throughout this book as Beijing, 'North Capital', even though it did not really gain that distinction until 1403.

1

The Land of Swallows

Only a hundred years ago, Zhoukoudian was still an obscure mining community on the outskirts of Beijing, where residents quarried the nearby limestone hills. One cliff, known as Chicken Bone Hill, was notorious for its endless supply of old animal remains. Nor were its artefacts always readily recognised – it also contained many fossils of unidentified creatures, written off by local authorities as 'dragon bones'.

Zhoukoudian doesn't attract the same dutifully trudging crowds as the Forbidden City. There are no truant students here trying to press-gang me into looking at their art show. No old ladies push postcards or souvenir fans. Zhoukoudian is a way out from the modern urban centre and chiefly of interest to archaeologists. On the day that I arrive, the car park is deserted. I have the gift shop to myself, the road to the summit is deserted, and at its terminus, I am the only man in the cave where the first men once dwelt.

A few foreign archaeologists picked over the area in the early twentieth century and carted off some debris to analyse. It was not until 1926, in Sweden, that scientists picking over some Zhoukoudian junk made the discovery of a lifetime – two human teeth. The first documented case of *Homo erectus pekinensis*, or 'Peking Man' had already travelled thousands of miles from the place where he, his ancestors and his distant descendants had made their home for tens of thousands of years.

A wide, clean road leads up the hill to the museum, flanked by memorial tablets to the scholars who excavated Peking Man and his artefacts – men such as John Gunnar Andersson, the Swedish geologist who surveyed the hill in 1918, Pei Wenzhong, the Chinese archaeologist who found the first skull in 1929, and Pierre Teilhard de Chardin, the French palaeontologist who would find greater fame in later life when he would be denounced by the Catholic church as a heretic.

A path winds away from the low, unobtrusive museum around the hilltop itself, where cavemen spent thousands of years looking down on the valley below. A single glance is not enough to appreciate its full impact. It is not the fact that I am in a cave that is impressive, but the fact that primitive man lived here for thousands of years. This bare cavern could be the very place where fire was first kindled; where the first words were spoken, where the first art was created in China. Like the Great Wall, it is not so much the sight itself that is humbling; it is the knowledge of how far it extends beyond view, out past the horizon, across the mountains and far back into time.

Time, not mere hours and days, but *geological* time, has changed this environment. A once-great river, where Peking Man fished and paddled, has shifted hundreds of miles to the south. Many of the caves have been carefully torn apart in the interests of science, and are only now being restored to their previous state. But *which* previous? Here there was once a soaring, vaulted hall of shadows, the limestone walls sweating with spring water, a place used by generation upon generation of animals in search of a safe den. Millennia later, it was a split-level caveman apartment, its lower reaches used for burials and refuse.

Standing at the lowest point of the Zhoukoudian excavations, you gaze upward at a towering rock face, layers marked with occasional numbers. What was once a great cavernous fissure, as high as a football pitch is long, has slowly filled up over the centuries. At its lowest level, there is nothing save scattered lumps of ancient hyena faeces, scuffed and ground into the rock. But after thousands of years of occasional hyena habitation, the cave gains a new coating of red silt, as if new rains have washed mud from a new river somewhere nearby. Amidst the sandy clay are pieces of human fossil, animal bones and pieces of stone worked into scrapers and primitive axes.

Five hundred thousand years ago, Peking Man had arrived. The area was a lush, secluded valley, rich in game and plants. Peking Man hid from leopards, sabre-toothed tigers and bears, in an environment that was a home to porcupines, woolly rhinoceros and gazelles. He hunted these animals, luring them into a cave with a sudden vertical drop where he could finish them off at his leisure, cooking their carcasses on the first fires, scraping their skins to make the first rudimentary clothes. 'Suddenly', if there can be a suddenly in geological time, Peking Man lost his furry covering and become a naked ape in need of animal skins to keep out the cold. He had become Upper Cave Man – *Homo sapiens*. Us.

Some have been harsh about Peking Man's culture. He has been accused of being a scavenger, not a hunter. His rudimentary, 'chopping' stone tools have been unfavourably compared with the 'axes' of his European cousins, although recent academic discourse has recognised that the easy availability of bamboo in China probably led to much more sophisticated tools that rotted away many centuries ago.

It has been suggested that he did not master fire quite as early as some believed. Forty per cent of the human remains at Zhoukoudian are those of children under 14 years of age. Only 2.6 per cent made it to fifty. His living arrangements have been ridiculed by modern observers who note not the fact of his survival, but the seemingly endless centuries in which so little changed, and early man huddled in the drafty, smoky gloom, chewing on the dirty, half-burnt, half-raw carcasses of bats.[1]

One day, the sky fell in. The roof collapsed, leaving half the former cave open to the sky. The tribe of Peking Man relocated to the caves which still offered some protection from the outside world. He lived there for another eleven thousand years.

There is something truly daunting about the history of Beijing – a place inhabited by mankind since before they were men, for literally hundreds of thousands of years. Ruins on the landscape mark the places where ancient reasons for habitation have disappeared – mighty rivers have changed their courses, and place-names recall the locations of dead springs, dried-up lakes and forgotten boundaries. There are hills in the Beijing area made by human hand; using soil and rocks dragged up to make great lakes. Beijing is the place where sub-human savages fought with bears and hyenas for shelter in mountain caves, where some of the first men hid from beasts now extinct.

When the distant descendants of Peking Man were able to talk, they told stories about their ancestors. The Chinese sage Confucius, among others, recognised that the ancestors of the Chinese had lived like beasts, cowering in the dark from the winter cold, and sleeping in trees during the summer heat:

> Formerly the ancient kings had no houses. In winter they lived in caves which they had excavated, and in summer in nests, which they had framed. They knew not yet the transforming power

of fire, but ate the fruits of plants and trees, and the flesh of birds and beasts, drinking their blood and swallowing [also] the hair and feathers. They knew not yet the use of flax and silk, but clothed themselves with feathers and skins.[2]

The traditional centre of Chinese civilisation was far to the south in Luoyang, deep along the valley of the Yellow River. But the Beijing region retained an important role in early Chinese folklore. It was, after all, inhabited for a long time. Thirty thousand years before the present day, Beijing was the place where Ice Age glaciers reached their southernmost moraine. It was the edge of the known world, looking southward to the plains of agrarian civilisation and north into the mountains, steppes and forests of the wilderness. According to legend, it was where man first tried to tame the elements, particularly fire and water.

There is a precarious cast to life on China's central plains. The Yellow River's floodplain stretches for hundreds of miles, creating a volatile environment in which the river can all too easily change course. Some of the 'smaller' rivers in north China have at times been part of the main course of the Yellow River, while some canals were actually dredged along the beds of forgotten former channels. Nor is water management a catch-all solution – the vast quantities of silt that give the river its hue and name are easily dumped on its bed and banks, allowing the river to spring over dams and break through levees, to the great danger of communities along its length. The result created a fear and respect for the mighty river throughout the time of Chinese legends.

The Beijing plain was almost uninhabitable for many centuries. The river's retreat turned the lowlands into a brackish marsh that stretched for many miles towards the sea, where reeds rocked in the wind across a long expanse of treacherous boggy ground. This, said the ancient legends, was the Waste of the Bitter Sea, home of a family of man-hating dragons, who poisoned the surrounding area in an attempt to hold humans at bay. These dragons pop up on several occasions in Beijing's history, taking the blame for local natural disasters or reversals of fortune. Long into recorded history, Beijing's struggle for fresh water frequently elicited comments about the dragons in its midst, who must be opposed, appeased, avoided.

Chinese mythology is a garbled mass of stories about ancient conflicts between godlike beings and earthbound tribes. Amid the slow expansion of numerous animal-totem tribes, two warring factions eventually signed a truce. A man called the Yellow Sovereign,[3] regarded by posterity as the ancestor of all the Chinese, led a confederation of totems, largely named after types of bear and big cat. They joined forces with another group, the *Shennong* people, quite possibly an alliance of nomad herders with pastoral farmers. This new confederation ran into another tribe somewhere in northeast China, where they fought over the precious resources of the plain of the Yellow River. Accounts differ as to the identity of the rival leader. Some call him Shennong, using the name of the tribe with which the Yellow Sovereign's people had already merged. Others name him Chi You, and call him a son of Shennong. Whoever this individual was, he is said to have led over seventy different tribes into battle.

Ancient Chinese texts describe Chi You as a veritable demon, with horns on his head and fleshy bat-wings that allowed him to fly, leading an army of giants, Koreans and evil spirits. His 81 brothers supposedly had the power of human speech, but the bodies of beasts. To hear them described, they sound more like tanks, with bronze skulls, iron foreheads, and a diet of rocks and stones. He had the power to transform his appearance, and magical powers that permitted him to command the wind and rain in his service. Legend recounts that they met in a single colossal battle, although the events described go on for literally weeks and months.

The Yellow Sovereign charged onto a battlefield obscured by a magical mist, and was forced to fall back on sorceries of his own. He used a magnetic device to determine directions (said to be the world's first compass), and employed the services of his daughter, Drought Fury, to somehow desiccate the air. Even then, the battle was not over. Chi You himself was hunted down by the dragon Yinglong, who killed him, and was cursed to remain forever on Earth in punishment. The scattered remnants of Chi You's people fled far to the southwest, where, many generations later after many migrations, they became the peripheral tribes known in Vietnam as the Hmong. To this day, Chi You is worshipped by the Hmong as a war god, and their term for him, pronounced in their own dialect as *Txiv Yawg*, means grandfather-ruler.

All this supposedly happened some time around 2500 BC, on the plains where Beijing now stands. As the capital of the Yellow Sovereign, this legendary (and archaeologically unknown) Beijing was a symbol of the order that the Yellow Sovereign brought to Earth, walls against the elements and channels dug to carry water.

The story of the Yellow Sovereign is deep in water symbolism – spirits of rain, drought and flood warring for control of a world – the mighty torrents of the Yellow river perhaps rebelling against the farmers who thought they had tamed them. Not for nothing is the unpredictable river sometimes known as China's Sorrow, in memory of the millions killed by its sudden shifts in direction. But with the Yellow River turning away from its former course, the region became less important.

But even if this legendary Beijing were a real place, it was soon marginalised in the eyes of the Chinese. The descendants of the legendary Yellow Sovereign moved ever westwards, eventually settling far upstream. Although the region where Beijing now stands was regarded as part of China by the earliest Chinese, it was still on the edge of the world. As the legendary divinities of antiquity began their slow segue into a list of historical kings, north-east China became one of a handful of dukedoms that paid fealty to the kings of the Zhou dynasty.

There is another forgotten conflict, unrecorded in the Chinese histories, but apparent from place-names. Where solid ground met marshland and lakes, facing the plains of reeds stretching far into the distance, there was a village called *Ji*, the Place of Thistles. Its inhabitants were eventually absorbed into another group, the Yan – a picturesque name meaning The Swallows.

The Place of Thistles became a community within the Land of Swallows, named for the flocks of darting birds that can still be seen turning in its skies. Ji remained a town within the Yan domains, but a few hundred years later the conqueror's capital was abandoned. Perhaps it was indefensible from northern barbarians, perhaps another well dried up, or floodwaters rose. Whatever the reason, Ji enjoyed a new lease of life – for the first time, the place we now call Beijing was the capital of a country.[4]

These people of the Swallow made their home in and among the people of the Place of Thistles. *Ji* became *Yan Jing*, the Capital of the Swallows; a poetic name that can still be found sometimes on products and services in the Beijing area.[5]

Its capital, identified from a handful of bronze artefacts unearthed to the south-west of modern Beijing, was small enclosure, barely 850 metres across, encircled by a rammed earth rampart.

Archaeology has determined that the site itself was larger, perhaps two miles across, implying that the original fort soon attracted settlers who built their homes outside its walls.

The Land of Swallows was originally founded as a border-march – a place where a military garrison might watch the mountains for signs of barbarian invaders from the north. The Great Wall of China began life in the north of the Land of Swallows, although in a far less majestic incarnation than the one known today. Despite such potential dangers north of its borders, there were many periods in the history of the region where the barbarians were amenable, contained, absent or simply otherwise occupied. During such years, the state of Yan was widely regarded as a paradise, insulated by its peripheral location from much of the diplomatic pushing and shoving of other early Chinese states. It was also blessed with good natural resources. Even the mountains on its northern border could be refashioned as south-facing agricultural slopes.

Su Qin, a famous diplomat from the nearby Land of Latecoming, once observed that the Land of Swallows enjoyed such an abundance of wild fruits and berries, that its citizens could live for months on end without troubling themselves over farming and harvests. Such a comment, if anything more than a bit of political flattery, could reflect the tail-end of the prehistoric cornucopia that may have first attracted Peking Man to the region. Yan was the weakest of the seven states, but its alliance was highly prized for the security it could offer for moving troops to other borders, contributing to war efforts, and protecting the flanks of its neighbours.[6]

It was widely believed, particularly among politicians, that China was on the threshold of a new era. With the ancient lineage of the Zhou kings now exercising little power beyond the walls of their own capital, true power lay with the dukes. China was fated to enter another cycle of civil war, and that after a indeterminate period of fighting, a single monarch would rise to subdue and unite the warring factions.

The Land of Swallows was spared much of the strife of the Warring States – the main culprit behind the wars of the fourth century BC was the distant Land of Qin, that dared not send an army against the Land of Swallows for fear that other countries would use the opportunity to attack it from the rear. Over the years, however, the men of Qin won battle after battle, and as the borders of the distant state expanded, they grew ever closer to the Place of Thistles.

Two countries were on a collision course. One was the aforementioned land of Qin, a harsh regime in the east, run on military lines and geared for permanent war. The other was Qi, the Land of the Devout, directly to the south of the Land of Swallows, determined to become the hegemon of the assembled kings, and thereafter the new ruler of all under heaven.

During the fourth century BC, the dukes of China cast off their loyalty to the powerless kings of the Zhou dynasty. Instead, each proclaimed himself a king in his own right. Duke Yi (r. 332–21) proclaimed that the Land of Swallows was no longer a vassal domain, but a fully independent monarchy. For the last two years of his reign, he was not a duke, but Beijing's first king, and his bold proclamation ushered in 101 years of monarchy, an eventful century that saw wildly fluctuating fortunes for northeast China.

Despite their claims of independence, most of the rulers of the former dukedoms entertained some hope that they would not merely prosper themselves, but dominate the others. They sought not to forget the Zhou kings of old, but to become just like them, absorbing their neighbours through means fair or foul, until one single autocrat dominated 'all under heaven' once more. The victor in that century of struggle would be the distant land of Qin to the west, the homeland of Duke Yi's wife. Cut off in its own remote valley, the state of Qin nurtured a project that was literally decades in the making, designed to create the perfect ruler, a ruthless conqueror devoid of any thought but domination, ruling an unstoppable state run on harsh and military discipline. The culmination of that bloodline would be born in 246 BC, and is remembered as the First Emperor of China. But in the hundred years that would pass before his victory over the Warring States, the other kingdoms jockeyed among themselves.

Even though it was stuck in its obscure corner, the Land of Swallows was soon embroiled in the kind of intrigues that characterised the period. With the death of its first king, his mourning period was not even officially over before the Land of Swallows was attacked by the neighbouring Land of the Devout, in a swift raid that seized ten cities on the countries' mutual borders. Su Qin was immediately dispatched as an envoy to the Land of the Devout, where he offered his congratulations to the king, and in the same breath, his condolences.

The king of the Land of the Devout was not expecting such a response, and pursued the ambassador across the throne room with a spear, demanding an explanation. Fearlessly, Su Qin told his enemy of what might happen. The Land of Swallows was indeed weak, but its marriage alliance with Qin gave it a friend in need – the leader of the most powerful and fearful army in the known world. The Land of Devout had snatched territory from its neighbour, engulfing it like a starving man grabs for food, but Su Qin warned his enemy that the territory he had just taken would be more like a deadly poison for the enemy who devoured it.[7]

The story we have is from the *Intrigues of the Warring States*, a book emphasising the wily nature of diplomatic discourse. But Su Qin's dialogue with the Land of the Devout is wholly believable. Whatever he said to his enemy, it was enough to make the Land of Devout return the territory, pay extensive damages, and offer a profound apology to both the Land of Swallows and its Qin allies.

Su Qin's younger brother Su Dai performed a similar role for King Kuai (r. 320–14). He, too, hoped to maintain the position of the Beijing region through intrigues, not military might. Su Dai was easily the match of his brother in such intrigues, and a consummate salesman, unafraid to put the tricks of pedlars and merchants to use in a courtly context. He was particularly fond of an old parable about a man trying to sell a fine horse, who stood, frustrated, in a marketplace for three days, without attracting any attention. For Su Dai, the quality of the horse might be of importance in a battle, or in a race, but it would not necessarily attract buyers in a market. The man in the parable eventually paid someone to shill for him, loudly 'noticing' the horse, praising its attributes, and lamenting that he wished he had the money to buy it, in order to attract actual customers. It was this sales trick, one of the earliest cases of viral marketing, that Su Dai was determined to put to use on potential rivals in the Land of the Devout.

When the Land of the Devout 'invited' minor Yan royals to visit, Su Dai advised his ruler to send them willingly – they might be hostages in all but name, but they would also be long-term guests, more liable to form friendships and political connections than to make enemies. Su Dai suggested that this would be even easier if Yan supplied the visitors with gold, silver and fine artefacts, so that they could bribe, impress and cajole their hosts.

The *Intrigues of the Warring States* record Su Dai's plans paying off in several diplomatic coups. Once, before arriving in the Land of the Devout for an important summit, he directly asked a Qi official if the man would play the part of the eager horse-buyer, planting stories and praises of Su Dai's greatness in the court, ready to make his arrival all the more impressive. Of course, Su Dai offered to pay his newfound friend's expenses, offering him a thousand measures of gold as 'horse's fodder.'

But ultimately Su Dai's prime loyalty was to himself, and his machinations would cause trouble for the Land of Swallows, particularly regarding his brother-in-law Zizhi, on behalf of whose promotion he was happy to play the part of the over-excited horse trader. Thanks to Su Dai and Zizhi, the Land of Swallows became a laughing stock among the Warring States, as the site of a supposed experiment in enlightened government, which ended in disaster.

The aging King Kuai lasted barely six years before he decided to abdicate his position – possibly through a combination of bad omens, bad luck and bad advice. Like many ministers during the Warring States era, Zizhi prized the message of an ancient folktale, in which the Yellow Sovereign's great great-grandson had determined that the ideal person to take over his kingdom was not his biological heir, but his wisest minister. With the help of Su Dai, Zizhi persuaded the old King that the way to score the ultimate publicity coup against the Land of Devout, to shame them for all eternity and blind them with virtue, was to nominate Zizhi as his heir.

The other countries, it was argued, could not fail to be impressed with the Land of Swallows, whose ruler would become the first in recorded history to directly emulate the sage-kings of legend. Just as they had held off military might with words, surely such a decision would put them ahead in the race to be recognised as the rightful ruler of the world?

King Kuai had his doubts, but was assured that this, too, was another ruse. Zizhi pointed out that all the main ministers were supporters of the Crown Prince, and that of course, behind the scenes, the Crown Prince would still wield real power. The appointment of Zizhi as the new king would simply be an exercise in showmanship, for the greater good of the Land of Swallows.

It was a disaster. No sooner had King Kuai abdicated, Zizhi and his supporters did just as they pleased. Their reign lasted for barely three years before it was confronted with a mass uprising in the Land of Swallows, comprising not just members of the general population, but also a large faction within the army, unsurprisingly in cahoots with the dispossessed Crown Prince.

While the rival factions were fighting each other, the wily Land of the Devout saw its chance, and sent its own army unopposed across the border. By the time the dust had settled, the usurpers were dead, but much of the Land of Swallows was under enemy occupation. After another year, the neighbouring Land of Latecoming, living up to its name, sent in its own forces, chasing out the invaders, and placing the hapless prince on the throne, as King Zhao (r. 311–279)

King Zhao had become the ruler of a land in ruins, and would never forgive the Land of the Devout for its opportunism. Nor was he particularly enamoured with the Land of Latecoming, a vassal state of distant Qin. An earlier ruler of the Land of Latecoming had assassinated a rival by smashing his skull in with a specially designed drinking goblet. It was, consequently, something of a racial stereotype that men of the Land of Latecoming were untrustworthy, two-faced brutes that were guaranteed to have ulterior motives. As King Zhao's new advisers saw it, his only hope of holding off an unwelcome return by his 'allies' from the Land of Latecoming was to go over their heads and contract an official alliance with his former enemy in Qin.

Another tale of the Warring States era credits Su Dai with the invention of a famous Asian folktale. He claimed to have seen a large mussel sunning itself on the banks of the River Yi that marked the border between the Land of Swallows and the Land of Latecoming. The mussel was attacked by a heron, and retaliated by slamming its shell shut, trapping the heron's beak. While the two animals remained locked in a stalemate, a passing farmer was able to catch them both. Su Dai likened the doubtful set-up of his fable to the constant warring of the minor states, and warned that Qin would be the sneaky farmer who stood to benefit from the strife.[8]

King Zhao's long reign was characterised by a single project – his desire for revenge against the Land of the Devout. Ultimately, he would oversee the organising of a coalition under General Yue Yi (another immigrant), which would pulverise the Land of the Devout in 284, invading on the flimsy pretext that the Land of the Devout had attacked an obscure statelet to its south. Unsurprisingly, its king had supposedly done so at the urging of a belligerent minister who had been bribed to suggest it by agents of the Land of Swallows!

General Yue Yi successfully persuaded his king not to attempt a unilateral invasion. The Land of the Swallows became a nominal partner in an international coalition. As the champion of the Land of Swallows, Yue Yi captured his enemy's capital, and brought home the greatest prize imaginable. The Great Regulator bell was an item of great magical power, property of the kings of old, and said to confer universal kingship on whoever possessed it. Like several other mythical artefacts, the Land of the Devout had acquired it as part of the preparations for conquering all rival kingdoms. Now, it was taken back to the Land of Swallows, and sat in King Zhao's palace.[9]

This gathering of the great and good, however, did not long outlast King Zhao himself, whose death in 279 was followed by purges and conspiracies that caused many of his greatest ministers and generals to flee to other countries. Even Yue Yi was not safe – slandered by an agent

of the Land of Devout, he fled the country, and
was living in exile when he heard the gratifying
news that his replacement had met with a
disastrous defeat at the hands of the resurgent
enemy. King Hui (r. 278–2) soon admitted his
failings in a pleading letter to Yue Yi, begging for
forgiveness from the official he had wronged,
citing unfamiliarity with his new
responsibilities, and a mistaken trust in his
officials as his excuses.

A better class of king might have served Yan
better, but the last ruler of the dynasty did not
learn from their mistakes. King Xi (254–22 BC)
repeated the errors of his ancestors. To the west,
the state of Qin's rolling conquest reached a
terrifying height in the neighbouring Land of
Latecoming, with a crushing defeat followed by a
mass execution of literally hundreds of thousands
of prisoners of war. Instead of regarding it as the
portent that it undoubtedly was, all King Xi
seems to have thought about was the opportunity
this afforded him to invade his ruined neighbour.
Just as his ancestor had ignored the counsel of
Yue Yi, King Xi disregarded the advice of one of
Yue Yi's descendants.

King Xi was ready for war, but this new
member of the Yue family advised against it,
refusing to consider an invasion even if his
allotted troops were tripled in number. The
angry king went ahead without him, and was
forced to apologise after the well-trained, battle-
hardened survivors of the massacre were able to
fight back the invasion.

Despite dynastic marriages that had ensured the rulers of the Land of Swallows and the Land of Qin were cousins of some description, the agents of Qin were still bent on conquering the known world. As the counts of the borderlands had been elevated to dukedoms, and then claimed kingship for themselves, one king was determined to proclaim himself as the ruler of All Under Heaven. Regardless of family ties, the Land of Swallows risked being engulfed by the armies of Qin. Beset by famine in his own country, still suffering the shame of an embarrassing defeat in another quarrel abroad, King Xi of the Land of Swallows was to be its last.

Tragically, King Xi had one of the best advisers of all. His own son and heir, the Red Prince, had actually been raised in Qin as one of the hostage-guests of the distant land. He had seen Qin's war machine at work first-hand, and had been a childhood friend of the man who was now Qin's ruler. King Xi, it seems, was content to replay the endless cycle of invasion and counter-attack, of insult and apology, which had characterised centuries of the Warring States. The king of Qin was playing an altogether different game, determined to proclaim himself as China's First Emperor.

More than two thousand years after the events described, it is difficult to assign blame. Possibly, King Xi was far more concerned about Qin than he cared to admit, but was placed in a position of plausible deniability by his own staff. But according to the historical record at least, King Xi had no part in the final solution of the Land of Swallows. Supposedly taking matters into his own hands, the Red Prince began a top-secret project designed to drive a knife into the heart of Qin's plans. Unable to put together a military force with the remotest chance of resisting Qin, he resorted to underhand methods. He initiated a project to put a suicidal assassin into the king of Qin's throne room with a poisoned dagger. The assassin would not make it out alive, nor would his assistant tasked with distracting the guards, nor would dozens of the Red Prince's agents, many of whom were killed off or poisoned to keep the project in the utmost secrecy. The assassin, a man called Jing Ke, lived for several years at the height of luxury and debauchery in the Land of Swallows, collecting, as it were, his payment in advance since he was unlikely to be alive to spend it afterwards.

Eventually, Jing Ke was dispatched to the land of Qin, travelling undercover as an ambassador from the Land of Swallows. Behind him, the slave-girls, entertainers and servants who had attended to him for so many months were likely already dead, along with many of the Red Prince's trusted and devout agents.

Jing Ke and his henchman were almost successful. After years of planning, months of travel, and days of waiting for the single perfect moment to strike, he got close enough to the king of Qin to snatch at his sleeve, diving for him with a dagger that he had kept hidden in a rolled-up scroll. But the king evaded his would-be killer, and the mission was a failure.[10]

Jing Ke's mission has achieved a legendary status in the centuries since. His ill-fated murder attempt was the last thing that stood between the days of feudal China and the initiation of the imperial era, for the king he failed to kill would soon become the First Emperor. But there is something strange about the mission. If it were that secret, how do we know about it?

Jing Ke did not make it out of the king of Qin's throne room alive. He died slumped against a pillar, struck repeatedly by the king with a massive ceremonial sword. Possibly, the story of the plot was extracted by torture from his henchman, whose fate is not recorded in the history books. But otherwise, the allegation that the Red Prince initiated the project is merely circumstantial.

Whether or not it was truly a top-secret plot by the Red Prince, Jing Ke's brief scuffle with the king of Qin was to spell the end of the Land of Swallows. Using the assassination attempt as a pretext, the army of Qin launched an assault on the Land of Swallows, using the Land of Latecoming as a staging post. By 226 BC, the capital of Yan had been occupied by Qin troops, and the last king of the Land of Swallows had fled to the northeast. Although fighting continued for several more years, the state of Yan was no more. King Xi appeased Qin by handing over a suitable scapegoat – the Red Prince's head was sent to Qin, and soon after, King Xi himself surrendered.

The Land of Swallows was gone, along with all the other states. All under heaven was now unified in a single political entity, ruled by the First Emperor. China was born.

2

North and South

北南

What had once been the Land of Swallows became a mere administrative district. The earthen rampart to the north of the Place of Thistles was strengthened and lengthened, eventually linking up with similar ramparts in the Land of Latecoming, to form the first incarnation of China's Great Wall.

The Land of Swallows was never truly a kingdom again, although later centuries occasionally raised ghosts of the past. A generation later, within a few months of the fall of the First Emperor's son, a rebel in the region proclaimed that the Land of Swallows lived once more. He was killed by another usurper, and within a couple of years, the resurgent kingdom had been re-incorporated into the empire. The Land of Swallows reappeared again in AD 27, when the local prefect briefly enjoyed two years as a self-crowned ruler. For much of the early Christian era, the ruler of the region enjoyed the status of a king (*wang*), although the meaning of the title had been devalued in imperial China, becoming more equivalent to our own 'prince'. Western China, closer to the new imperial capital at Luoyang, was ruled in a system of prefectures and provinces. Eastern China, including the Beijing area, was less tightly controlled, and often enjoyed a status more akin to tributary princedoms.

China's former kingdoms have never been forgotten. Throughout the imperial era, they remained in poetic allusions and administrative divisions. Chinese astrologers divided the sky itself into nine areas, each believed to be a heavenly parallel with its earthbound equivalent – activity in the Yan quadrant, be it meteors or supernovae, was sure to be tallied with troubles in the area marked by the former borders of the Land of Swallows.

At some point, the region was inundated with seawater once more, turning hundreds of square miles into marshland. Just one of many changes in local features, the flood let to the rechristening of the area as *Kuhai*, the Bitter Sea, and to local stories that blamed the problem on those angry local dragons, unwilling to allow human settlers into their domain. The mischievous spirits were usually depicted as a family of four – the Dragon King and his wife, son and daughter – and town planning in Beijing remained dominated by concerns of ensuring an adequate water supply.

Despite this, the region prospered, attracting foreign immigrants such as the Xianbei, who settled in the Beijing area and refused to budge. Chinese history has a habit of writing off all immigrants as 'barbarians' — conveniently forgetting the insult just as soon as the new arrivals have married into local families, adopted Chinese names, and settled down. Many parts of what is now called China were home to unique civilisations distinct from that of the 'Han' Chinese, but centuries of contact have diminished their local qualities. Today, there are but a few indicators of what were once very different cultures, such as the forked swords and alien statues of the native Sichuanese; the blunted, blocky pagodas that remain in the domain of the Xixia, the prominent Western noses of the descendants of Persian refugees in the hinterland, or the darker skin and Muslim faith of the inner Asian Uighurs. Similar cultural contacts appear to have been a feature of the Beijing region, where the local military developed a reputation for proficient cavalrymen, thanks largely to recruits from 'barbarian' immigrants like the Xianbei.

There are moments in the records where we can see the alien nature of Beijing life showing through. In the first century BC, three local men approached a magistrate from the south with a paternity dispute. The magistrate was aghast to discover that the three men all had the same wife, and scandalised when he realised that they had sought his aid because they had assumed he would regard their arrangement as completely normal. There were four children of this *ménage*, and the case turned on the question of who was whose. The magistrate observed that such questions of paternity and inheritance were precisely why Chinese tradition demanded a man should have a single wife, or at worst, a chief wife and many concubines. There was simply no provision in Chinese tradition for a single woman with many husbands, and such polyandry was regarded as a barbarian affront to Chinese decency. The shocked magistrate hence ordered the execution of the offending husbands, regarding their behaviour as 'inhuman'.[1]

Whether the ruler was a prefect or a governor, a prince or a 'king', he was powerful enough to bring major changes. The Bitter Sea was brought back under control, with a network of canals dug for proper irrigation. Some of the worst of the marshes were drained in public projects that clearly benefited all. When an earthquake in 294 damaged the network, everybody pitched in on repairs – even the Xianbei regarded by the central government as unwelcome immigrants.[2]

Perspectives, of course, differ. For many generations of Chinese emperors, the Beijing region remained a borderland, perilously close to the wild north, open to assault by any number of barbarian tribes. But life looked different in Beijing itself, where the barbarians were not a haunting, unknowable threat, but often relatives, trading partners, in-laws and friends. In what would be come a feature of Beijing life for over a thousand years, the region enjoyed a dual status, not just as a north-eastern outpost of 'traditional' Chinese civilisation, but as a south-eastern centre for the barbarian tribes. Not all were fierce nomads on horseback, although many were. To the average Western layman, it would be extremely different to tell a Beijing barbarian from a Beijing Chinese – they ate the same food, wore the same clothes, and argued about the same things.

For a sense of this largely forgotten element of northeast Asian culture, you need only go to a Russian restaurant and ask for 'Siberian dumplings'. It is something of a shock when one's order arrives, and comprises objects indistinguishable from Chinese *jiaozi*, lacking only Chinese condiments. The dumpling travelled both east and west from Central Asia in the early Middle Ages, along with the durum wheat that was a vital component of both it and noodles – neither is native to China, and yet both are commonplace on Chinese menus, particularly in 'Peking' restaurants. Rice remained relatively unpopular in the north until at least the end of the first millennium – paddy fields used up far greater quantities of precious water than the administration could really afford, while the largely cavalry-based military complained that the boggy ground of paddy fields proved difficult for their squadrons to cross at speed.

For a brief period in the AD 300s, the ruler of the Land of Swallows was once more able to claim that he was indeed a true king, but this sign of the wavering of imperial authority carried implications of its own. The emperor's power was failing beneath incursions from new western barbarians, and when these attackers reached Yan, its renewed independence was crushed beneath a new imperium.

We see traces of this new culture in one of China's most famous poems, the *Ballad of Mulan*. Known today chiefly for its use as an inspiration for a Disney film, our modern image of Mulan is based on riotously anachronistic artistic licence. Style in the cartoon often leans on Han dynasty carvings, whereas the Beijing depicted in the film's finale owes much of its architecture to the Qing dynasty. But Mulan's tale probably dates from the fifth or sixth century of the Christian era, when north China was under barbarian control.

Presented at first like a poem of lost love, it shows a girl sighing at her loom, only to reveal, to the great surprise of many a tavern audience, that she is not pining from romance, but from a desire to do her family proud by joining the army.

> Last night I saw the army notice
> The Khan calls up the soldiers
> Conscription lists in twelve scrolls
> And each one names a father.[3]

Since Mulan is an only child, there is no brother to take her father's place in the conscription rolls, and she resolves to disguise herself as a man and join up herself. But the magic word here is *Khan*, not emperor. Although Mulan later meets him in person, and he is described later in more traditional terms as the

'Son of Heaven', the man with whom she is dealing is clearly not a traditional Chinese ruler. She serves ten years in a prolonged campaign, in locations as far afield as the Yellow River and 'the Mount of Swallows', before a grateful Khan offers her a government position.

> The Khan asks for her desire [but]
> Mulan has no need of high office
> 'Just a sturdy camel
> To take me to my distant home.'[4]

The world in which the original Mulan serves is so alien to traditional China, so caught up in the Inner Asian worldview, that her mount of choice is a camel. And yet, she lives in a society advanced enough for her 'barbarian' town to possess four markets (a stylised description in verse five describes her shopping for her equipment), and organised enough to have roll-calls of conscripts. It is far removed from the Mulan of the Disney movie, who is shown *defending* China from such northern barbarians, who have climbed over the Great Wall and threaten the south.

Buddhism had also spread into China from India, and the new religion proved particularly popular among the northern tribes. In part, this may have been because they too saw themselves as new arrivals in a new land, but Buddhism also offered an escape route from the homespun, relentlessly parochial concerns of Chinese folk religion. This became particularly important in the early middle ages, when China was reunited under the Sui emperors, who immediately flung their nascent realm's limited resources into a foreign war with the Koguryo kingdom of northern Korea. In the Chinese fancy that life will imitate art, Beijing was renamed *Youzhou*, the Tranquil City, and functioned as the headquarters for a series of northward campaigns in the sixth and seventh centuries. The first campaigns were disastrous for China, and caused religious friction between Chinese popular religion and the Buddhism of the new aristocracy. Chinese folk beliefs held that the best possible life was lived at home, in harmony and tranquillity, and that a peaceful new existence awaited in the afterlife if one's corpse was safely returned to its hometown, buried with full honours, and appeased with regular ceremonial attention by one's ancestors.

This belief presented ample opportunity for religious dissent over the foreign wars of the new Sui emperors. Major defeats in Korea brought the Sui generals home, ready to fight another day, but they abandoned many thousands of their soldiers, left for dead on foreign fields, without proper burial, and with no hope of being transported home for the correct religious ceremony. The public backlash was a contributing factor to the swift demise of the Sui, overthrown by their cousins, the Tang dynasty, within a single generation.

Determined to avenge the Korean defeat, the Tang emperor Taizong arranged for Beijing to gain its first cenotaph in 645, the Temple of the Origin of the Law, where it was promised that monks would say prayers for the many war dead of the earlier campaigns. The founding of the temple was just one of several public relations exercises designed to bring the people around, but it failed to bring much luck to Taizong's armies. Fought to a standstill in Korea on a campaign of his own, he returned to his capital a broken man, and never quite recovered from the experience.[5] His successors were careful to appease both Buddhist and local beliefs, leading to several confusions. The most famous is probably the claim by the Empress Wu, who was a teenage concubine at the time of Taizong's death, that she was the earthly reincarnation of a Buddhist deity. But the clash of such different religious beliefs would also create new myths, one of which became part of Beijing's rich heritage.

Buddhism brought with it a menagerie of new gods and demigods, picked up during the religion's spread through India, and co-opting many old Hindu deities into its pantheon. By the time Buddhism arrived in China, translation into and out of at least one foreign language, if not too, had wrought serious shifts in the interpretation of many scriptures. The snake- and elephant-inspired *naga* creatures of Hindu myth were transformed in translation into Chinese as *long*, or 'dragons', creating a tidal wave of new dragon stories to confuse local folk religion.

These 'dragon' tales became mingled with parts of a local legend about a trickster god, to create a myth that became permanently interwoven with Beijing folklore. In the days before Chinese children were entertained by legends of the Monkey King, they heard about a child with super powers. After a long gestation period, Nezha was born to humble parents at an inauspicious hour of the morning. Cut from a fleshy sac by his irate father, the boy had three heads, each with a bonus central eye. He had eight hands, each wielding a golden weapon, and his whole body shone with an eerie red glow. Nezha could travel at great speed by riding on fiery wheels, and wielded a magic bracelet that could somehow crush foes with the force of the entire horizon. Although some myths of Nezha appear to date back to the second millennium BC, many of the tales seem to have been fashioned in medieval times. Suggestions, for example, that he was the shield-bearer to the ruler of Heaven, the Jade Emperor, probably date from the 800s, when the Jade Emperor was officially adopted as the patron deity of the Tang dynasty's ruling house.

One of the most famous tales about Nezha records his conflict with a local dragon, which took exception to the churning of the river waters while Nezha was doing his laundry. A boundary dispute soon turned into an argument about who really ruled the area's all-important water, and ended with Nezha lifting his magic bracelet (usually depicted as something more like a metal hoop) and slaying the dragon with a single blow. The other dragons demanded restitution, leading to a feud between Nezha's exasperated family and the all-powerful creatures. Eventually, Nezha committed suicide to save his parents from having to pay any reparations, but his troubles continued in the afterlife. His mother built a temple to his memory, hoping thereby to ensure that he would be reincarnated – a Buddhist ending, tacked on a Chinese folk tale. His angry father, still intensely irked with his son's wild life and ignominious death, tore the temple down, leading a local priest to fashion a new Nezha out of lily stalks and lotus leaves. Eventually, the spirit of Nezha would be given a military post in Heaven, and there, the confused story should end.[6]

However, over the centuries, the story of Nezha came to be associated specifically with the Beijing region, particularly in the later days of the Ming dynasty, when Nezha would offer supernatural aid to the citiy's architects. Although the location of the original stories seems sited in some vague dreamtime, the drift of the imperial family, Chinese religion and straightforward population numbers towards the north-east led many to assume that Nezha's story was bound to be associated with Beijing. But such assumptions would have to wait until the day that China was united once more.

For the four hundred years until 1368, Beijing was barely part of China at all. Its history went on, its trade continued, it stayed on the map, but its rulers were 'barbarians'. At the end of the Tang dynasty in 907, Khitan Tartars took control of north China, and Beijing with it. During this period, the ruins of the Great Wall defended the region from nobody. Nor was Beijing in the 'north' – in fact, in 938 it was renamed Nanjing ('South Capital') in recognition of its relation to other urban centres of the Liao dynasty – a ruling elite of Khitan tribesmen. Chinese history books of this period usually claim that China was under the rule of the Song dynasty, but while 'real' Chinese history bumbled merrily along in the south, and the emperors of the Song continued to call themselves the ruler of all under heaven, Beijing changed hands once more. Its new masters, in 1115 were a second Tartar tribe, the Jurchens, who ruled as the Jin ('Golden') dynasty until 1260, when they were ousted by still a third group of barbarians, the Mongols.

The names of the city continued to fluctuate. It was the south capital of the Liao, but was extensively enlarged and improved under the Jurchen, renamed the Holy Capital, 'Shengdu', and then the Middle Capital, 'Zhongdu' – a fair indication of the successful southern advance by the Jurchen armies, who marched as far south as the Yangtze.

China is a pragmatic civilisation. It works its magic on its oppressors, and it has time to do so. If Peking Man could exist for millennia in his caves, it takes but a blink of an eye for the

Chinese system to ensorcel its conquerors. The initial days of any conquest were surely violent and dangerous, but within a few years, the temptations were there to appeal to a ruler's sense of snobbery and self-worth. Chinese princesses reared the next generation of half-Tartar heirs, and the new rulers inherited a bureaucracy dominated by Chinese. Even if the belligerent conquerors had wanted to lose themselves in administration, there would never have been enough of them to go round. Despite their unquestioned military might and the unavoidable fact of their dominance, they still felt dwarfed by the cultural and historical heritage of the land they had conquered. It was not enough for them to rule this little piece of China, they wanted the whole thing, and it did not take long at all for them to hear of the Mandate of Heaven. If they wanted to gain Heaven's blessing for their planned conquest of the south, they would have to behave in a Chinese manner. Although the conquerors planned on clinging to their own religion, they were soon dragged into the seasonal cycle of the Chinese world, making sacrifices at the altars of Heaven and Earth, Sun and Moon. Tellingly, Beijing did not even possess such important sacred spaces – the Jurchen had to build them themselves, in imitation of those that they knew could be found far to the south in 'real' China.

Beijing's new masters had an inferiority complex about the 'true' Chinese capital to the south, ruled by the emperors of the Song.

Accordingly, they enlisted the services of Zhang Hao, a Chinese architect, to turn the city of 'Zhongdu' into a Chinese-style capital that outdid the real thing. The Song capital of Kaifeng had grown organically over the centuries. It had developed suburbs beyond the walls, and strange kinks in its shape due to natural landmarks. Compare that to Beijing under the barbarians, which was almost a perfect square, oriented on a north-south axis in perfect keeping with the stipulations of ancient tradition.

The designs and sacred buildings of Jurchen Beijing were deliberately designed to recall the idealised chronicles of the forgotten capital of the kings of the Zhou Golden Age. By 1153, the 'barbarian' ruler of the Jurchen was worshipping in a Chinese style at altars built to ancient designs, and keeping Chinese style ancestral tablets in order to pay homage to his forebears' spirits in special shrines.

He also adhered to Chinese superstitions. Although some temple pagodas might climb higher than a couple of stories, 99ft was usually regarded as the maximum height allowable by the principles of *feng shui*. Good spirits, supposedly, flew through the air at a height of 100ft, and any buildings in their airspace might impede their bestowal of fortune. As with so many explanations from Chinese geomancy, one is tempted to reverse cause and effect. It is, after all, far better to have the spirit world as an alibi, than it is to admit to a keen ruler that the tall buildings he wants in his own honour are liable to collapse, earthquake damage and diminishing returns in terms of inhabitability.[7]

Beijing under non-Chinese occupation also saw the reassessment of certain old legends, such as that of Draught Ox, a straight line of three stars in what we would call the constellation of Vega, and the Weaver Maid, a triangle of stars in what we would call the constellation of Altair. Although the constellations were two of many in the ancient Chinese sky, the fact that an ox-drover was male, and a weaver female, and that the two stars were separated by the 'river' of the Milky Way, led later centuries to append a tale of star-crossed lovers who would be able to meet only once a year, on the seventh day of the seventh month, when a bridge of magpies would form across the river that divided them. The story of the Draught Ox and the Weaver Maid took many centuries to develop, but became particularly popular during the period of Jurchen rule over Beijing. On the seventh day of the seventh month, courtiers in Jurchen Beijing would wear badges showing the magpie bridge, supposedly in homage to the traditional festival, although possibly also out of a deep-seated sense of separation from the rest of China, south of the Jurchen border, eternally waiting for a fantastical remedy.[8]

During the period of Khitan and Jurchen domination, Beijing's population seemed obsessed with other cities, particularly the life they imagined was going on far to the south, in a

China that was not under foreign rule. Thoughts were on romantic idylls of an idealised, peaceful existence under the Song, or military schemes, eternally plotted and redrafted, for an eventual takeover. Chinese on both sides of the border speculated about reunification, and as the barbarian ruling class was diluted with increasing amounts of Chinese blood with every generation, the separation of these two Chinas seemed increasingly ludicrous. By the thirteenth century, the standoff between the Northern Jin and Southern Song was no longer a matter of a slow invasion, whose frontline had remained static for more than a century. Instead, it had become a contest between two rival dynasties for the favour of Heaven. North and South both strove to outdo each other in the ostentation of their religious services, and with their capitals' claims to be the Centre of the World. Such boasts were not made to each other in diplomatic communications, but directly to Heaven, in a constant struggle for a sign, some portent or astrological manifestation, that China would soon be unified once more. As part of this one-upmanship, the denizens of Beijing clung to their own ancient history, particularly Beijing's brief period as a monarchy, and the dimly remembered legends of ancient prominence. Even when the capital of China was far to the south, the people of the Beijing region still assured each other that the land where they lived and died had been the site of ancient clashes between gods and demons, and (ironically with some element of truth), where men had first walked the earth.

A folk tale of the period maintains a sense of yearning for a lost unity with the south, subtly buried beneath a traditional love story. The association of the area with the swallow continued, particularly with reference to the Terrace Where Swallows Muster, an earth mound in the countryside outside modern Beijing, where thousands of birds congregated each autumn. Flocks of swallows sufficient to darken the sky stay in the area for a few days, before beginning their winter migration south, to Hainan and points beyond. The sight of the birds, however, eventually generated a legend of its own, redolent of tragic medieval romances, Grimm's fairy tales and even a touch of Oscar Wilde, in the story of a rich landlord's daughter.

So the story goes, Hongbao ('Ruby') was persecuted for her innocent friendship with the son of a poor man. Despite her protestations that Xiao Yan ('Little Swallow') was just a friend, the girl was ordered never to see him. Her carefree childhood play was curtailed as she reached marriageable age, and she was no longer permitted to go outside. Imprisoned indoors with nothing to do but embroider, she amused herself by occasionally ditching the flower patterns she had been provided, in favour of small and exquisite thread birds, which she would drop out of the window as gifts for Xiao Yan.

Her father hears her whispering 'Fly, swallow! Fly away!' and immediately assumes the worst.

So might we, but centuries of fairytale retellings have reversed the likely truth of the tale — instead, we are told that one of her embroidered birds had come to life, and it was that which she was addressing. Her scandalised father, however, will not be persuaded, and instead bribes a local magistrate to exile Xiao Yan far to the south on trumped-up charges.

As Ruby pines away for her lost beau, she is visited by a lone bird, returning from the distant tropical island, and tweeting the worst news that she can imagine: that Xiao Yan has died in exile. Ruby asks the bird to confirm by flying three times around her house, which it then does. Ruby then cries herself to sleep, weeping tears of blood — standard Chinese hyperbole for misery, but here taken literally. When she inevitably dies of a broken heart, she is buried up on the earthen slope near her house — a place that soon grows with strange 'Swallow Grass', whose blood-red sap can be squeezed out and used to make dyes and cosmetic rouge. Thereafter, each year, the swallows return to the terrace and wait for two days in the vicinity of the grave, in case the spirit of Ruby has a message for them to take south to Hainan.[9]

North and South would eventually be reunited, but not through any Chinese or supernatural agency. In the thirteenth century, the North was conquered by a new tribe of outsiders — the Mongols. Beijing put up a brave resistance to the approach of Genghis Khan — brave because the Mongols famously offered no quarter to any who refused to surrender. By not immediately opening its gates to the Mongols, Beijing's fate was sealed, and the city succumbed to a relentless storm of fire-arrows in 1215. The Mongols, their forces swelled by defecting Chinese soldiers who had originally been tasked with defending the city, crashed through the gates and put every living thing in the city to the sword. The surviving palaces were looted and set on fire, and by the time the army had passed, Beijing had been totally destroyed.

3

Khanbalikh

大都

A surviving report of the immediate aftermath paints a terrifying picture. The firestorm reduced the buildings of Beijing to charred ruins, while men, women and children had died in such huge numbers that the streets were slick with human fat. Beijing was left to the buzzards, and remained a ghost town for several decades, until Khubilai, the grandson of Genghis Khan, completed the conquest of China, uniting the country for the first time in centuries, and proclaiming himself the first emperor of a new dynasty, which he gave the majestic and provocative title of *Yuan*: Beginning.

This new beginning solved the enduring problem of the rival capitals in North and South. The new ruler chose the location of the true capital. He chose Beijing.

When Khubilai Khan's architects began constructing what would be known as Khanbalikh, 'the Khan's city', they ignored the blackened, haunted shell of the old town, and built a completely new one on its northeast corner. The new city's most famous European resident, the Venetian merchant Marco Polo, wrote that Khubilai's astrologers had predicted the old town would rebel, and so encouraged him to weasel out of the curse by *building* nearby instead of *rebuilding* the site itself.[1]

But while such folktales may have made for amusing fireside anecdotes in local taverns, they ignored more prosaic reasons for the move. The ruined city could have easily been restored, but the Mongols were planning for a much bigger metropolis. Beijing had been the meeting place of north and south for many centuries, but now Khubilai Khan was to proclaim himself as a Chinese emperor, the first of the new Yuan dynasty, he would need more than just a regional capital. He needed a national capital, and with such a plan came the expectation of a much larger urban population. Khubilai's city soon grew into one of the largest in the world, laid out with wide regular avenues that impressed all foreign visitors. The most famous contemporary account of the city is that of Marco Polo, who wrote of the city of 'Cambaluc' in his *Travels*.

All the plots of ground on which the houses of the city are built are four-square and laid out with straight lines; all the courts and gardens or proportionate size. . . . Each square plot is encompassed by handsome streets for traffic, and thus the whole city is arranged in squares just like a chess board. . . . In the middle of the city there is a great [bell] which is struck at night. And after it had struck three times, no one must go out of the city.[2]

The 'chess-board' pattern of the Mongol city, as reported by Polo, remained such a feature of Beijing geography that locals still navigate by the points of the compass. North, south, east and west are regularly employed in street names and directions imparted to travellers in the modern era – it is virtually impossible to get lost in old Beijing. Exit any alleyway onto a boulevard, and you can immediately work out your location in relationship to the centre of town.

Polo was able to get a bird's eye view of the city by climbing the steps to the roof of one of the city's eleven gates (he counted twelve, but close enough). The city was smaller in those days, and smog-free, and Polo was able to see clear across to the opposite wall – the avenues were straight all the way.

The dragons of the Bitter Sea, those recurring characters of Beijing legend, would also have their say. The water supply for the old city was simply too paltry to support Khubilai's plans. It was far better for the Mongols to site their new capital on at the northeastern edge of the old town, where two rivers flowed into an elongated pair of lakes, the site of a previous royal park, before continuing on their way out of town. Khubilai's personal palace was built on the eastern shore of one of these lakes, which was dredged and expanded – the soil and rocks from the process dumped to the north to form the basis of what is now Coal Hill to the north of the Forbidden City.

One of the few remnants of the Mongol era survives in what is now Beihai Park where the serene and most northerly lake curves gracefully around Hortensia Island, once the private preserve of the Mongol emperors. Marco Polo described the park in its Yuan dynasty heyday as a paradise:

> Between the two walls of the enclosure are fine parks and beautiful trees bearing a variety of fruits. There are beasts also of sundry kinds, such as white stags and fallow deer, gazelles and roebucks, and fine squirrels. . . There extends a fine Lake, containing fish of different kind which the Emperor has caused to be put there, so that whenever he desires any he can have them at his pleasures. A river enters this lake and issues from it, but there is a grating of iron or brass put up so that the fish cannot escape in that way.[3]

But Polo may never have seen the park for himself, or if he did, only on a brief escorted visit. He does, however, have plenty to say about other pleasures on offer elsewhere in the city, and claims that Yuan-era Beijing boasted some 20,000 prostitutes.[4]

Place names and folklore retain vestiges of many a drunken night in Beihai Park. Several *trees* in the park were awarded ministerial rank in old imperial governments, doubtless conferred upon them by sozzled rulers. Although a bridge now connects Hortensia Island to the rest of the park, in Khubilai's time it was only reachable by boat. A day in the park would end with boating on the lake in the sunset, and at dusk, all the barges would be moored at the island, and the khan and his followers could spend the night with their women in a number of exquisite pavilions. For any consort who had managed to run a gauntlet of obstructive eunuchs and imperial caprices, a night trapped on Hortensia Island was a coveted opportunity; for any Yuan-dynasty beauty that did not want the attentions of an amorous emperor, it was a nightlong test of endurance.

The park was not always as tranquil as it seems today. Beijing folklore retains a story that may be the vestiges of a forgotten murder, or simply a groundless bogeyman to scare children. But, so the stories go, sometimes a black-cloaked man can be found in Beihai Park, offering to take late-night loiterers home. Instead of being a friendly old-world taxi driver with a donkey cart, the man is actually a ghost, determined to drag unsuspecting passengers down into his lair beneath the bridge, where he drowns them in the waters of the lake and feeds on their souls.[5]

Resident in Beijing sometime in the 1280s, Marco Polo was a *semuren* – a 'colour-eyed man' – one of many hundreds of foreign administrators employed by the Mongols to aid in running their newly conquered country. Most of the *semuren* were from Central Asia, and their number included many Nestorian Christians and Muslims, leading to certain anxieties at the capital. Matters were particularly tense over the subject of religion – missionaries from all major faiths, as well as a number of cultists and outright charlatans, were honoured guests at

Khubilai's court, and kept permanently guessing as to the emperor's disposition towards them. All lived in hope that the Mongol conqueror would recognise their belief as the one ultimate truth, and drag the people of China along with him in his conversion. But Khubilai hedged his bets throughout his reign, refusing to come out for or against any one religion. His chief wife was a Nestorian Christian, most of his advisers Buddhists or Muslim, but Khubilai himself was careful to appeal to everyone.

The Mongols dwelt in the newly built area or 'Tartar City', while the old ruins and the formerly unoccupied land soon filled up with their subjects – the ruins were not abandoned for long, but soon attracted entrepreneurs and merchants who wiped out most traces of the old city. Few Mongols and fewer of the foreign *semuren* administrators were fluent in Chinese, and most communications among Marco's colleagues was conducted in Persian. It seems that Marco himself never learned more than a few words of Chinese, leading to many supposed 'errors' in his account of his travels. In fact, his experience of China was akin to that of a foreign diplomat on a brief fact-finding mission, forced to regard everything through the limited opportunities afforded for actual local contacts.

The centuries of north-south divide in China had created palpable differences, enough for Marco Polo to believe that China was two countries – 'Khitai', where Beijing could be found, and 'Manzi' to the south. Ironically, the latter term was actually Chinese for 'southern barbarian', co-opted by the occupied north as a derogatory term for China proper.[6] There are tantalising hints in Polo's account that someone sat him down on at least one occasion and attempted to explain how Beijing had been subject to non-Chinese rule for some time before the arrival of the Mongols. However, the story was easily garbled – determined to make themselves sound legitimate, the Jurchens had given their dynasty a Chinese name: *Jin*. As it literally means 'Golden', Polo seems to have confused this period (1115–1234) with an unrelated *Jin* kingdom from two thousand years previously, and the close pronunciation of *Qin*, the dynasty of the First Emperor. This caused him to relate fanciful and muddled tales of a legendary 'Golden King' in the region, that were linked, probably by his own wishful thinking, to other stories of the fabled Christian king of Asia, Prester John.[7]

Modern writing on China often implies a racially homogenous population, but although the Han Chinese are a dominant ethnic group, there are many minorities. Polo's description of the Khan's realm includes discussions of Muslim peoples, primitive tribes in the jungles, Indians, Tibetans and Turks. On rare occasions when Polo did deal directly with the 'real' Chinese, he often found them infuriating – particularly the women, who were demure, graceful and entirely unavailable.

The most important development for Beijing during Marco Polo's time was the renovation of its Grand Canal. At first, the Mongols expected that grain fleets sailing up the coast of China, into the Gulf of Bohai and then upriver near what is now Tianjin could feed Beijing's hungry mouths. Pirates aside, the greatest danger was the weather, culminating in a disastrous sequence of events in the famine year of 1286 when a quarter of the city's grain was lost at sea in storms.

Partly out of a deep-seated mistrust of the open sea, and partly from a pragmatic desire to avoid pirates and charge enforceable tolls, the Mongols ordered the construction of a canal that would connect Beijing to the south. Khubilai made the renovation (in fact, recreation) of the old Sui dynasty canal his top priority, and symbolically reunited North and South with a critical waterway for the first time in centuries. Chinese rulers had dredged river transportation corridors across the land before, but the Yuan dynasty saw a vast improvement. At the time of Marco's residence, the canal still stopped a way short of the metropolis itself, obliging merchants to offload their cargoes and wheel them the final few miles into Beijing on carts. Around 1293, shortly after Marco Polo left China for his European homeland, the canal network was extended right to Beijing itself.[8]

The canal made it possible for grain barges to come all the way from the fertile south from river system, to lake, to canal to river system, without once having to head for open water. It was now feasible to have a capital in the north that continued to grow – the Mongols had planned sufficiently ahead, and their new, larger water supply and better provisioning ensured that Beijing grew swiftly.

Transport networks were improved elsewhere, too. To the west of Beijing, Marco Polo described a buzzing market area, where a sturdy bridge complete with churning water mills became the site of a market area – with merchants unloading their goods ready for transhipment, but often hoping to save on cargo by selling them off right away.

> When you leave the City . . . and have ridden ten miles, you come to a very large river which is called Pulisangkin and flows into the ocean, so that merchants with their merchandise ascend to it from the sea. Over this river there is a very fine stone bridge, so fine indeed that it has few equals.[9]

The river was known as the Sanggan from the eighth century onwards, but this appears to be a coincidence. His *Pulisangkin* is not Chinese at all, but simply Persian for 'stone bridge'. The Chinese themselves called it the bridge of *Lugou* ('the Cottage/Black/Lu Family Waterway'), but today it is universally known outside China as the 'Marco Polo' Bridge.

> The fashion is this: It is 300 paces in length and it must have a good eight paces in width, for ten mounted men can ride across it abreast. It has 24 arches and many water mills, and is all of a very fine marble, well built and firmly founded. Along

the top of the bridge there is on either side a parapet of marble slabs and columns made in this way: At the beginning of the bridge there is a marble column, and under it a marble lion so that the column stands upon the lions loins while on top of the column there is a second lion both being of great size and beautiful sculpture. At the distance of a pace from this column, there is another precisely the same, also with its two lions and the space between them is closed with slabs of grey marble to prevent people from falling over into the water. And this the columns run from space to space along either side of the bridge, so that altogether it is a beautiful object.[10]

In the twenty-first century, the Marco Polo Bridge has been carefully renovated. Some original paving slabs are retained in its central walkway, but for show only, so that modern visitors can gaze in awe at the wear and tear done to hard stone by centuries of footfalls from litter-bearers, porters and cutpurses. Stone friezes and statues at either end tell tales about the bridge's history, but they are clearly modern additions. So, too, are many of the stone lions that first attracted Marco's attention. One only needs to look at the heads of the giant stone turtles, worn almost featureless by generations of attention from excited children, to see how a true Yuan-dynasty artefact is likely to look today.

The period of Mongol rule saw the construction of massive drum and bell towers to match the city's expanded size. The absence of any form of readily available time piece meant that the standard method of time keeping across the city, for merchants, priests and members of the public was defined by the sounding of the central towers. The drums were beaten in the morning to signify the start of the day; the bells rung at night to announce the formal end of the day – Beijing did not have a curfew as such, but anyone going out after the sounding of the Bell Tower would need a lantern to light their way, and a bodyguard to watch over them.

The Mongol Bell tower was built in 1272, and stood for nearly five hundred years before its destruction by fire and replacement with the one that stands today. But it is the Mongol tower that became part of Beijing's local folklore, its huge bell producing a surprisingly mournful, soft chime each evening, sounding to Chinese ears like someone whispering *xie, xie*.

Beijing children were told that it was time to go to bed, because the Bell Goddess was calling for her shoe (*xie*), a story that grew with the telling to become a tragic fairy tale of the bell's construction. An unnamed emperor (presumably Khubilai) ordered his Minister of Works to cast a ten-ton bell, but was displeased with the iron monstrosity that was first produced. He told his craftsmen to come up with a bronze replacement in just three months, big enough and loud enough for its sound to carry as far as Beijing's suburbs.

Working under pain of death, the craftsmen faced great difficulty with their enforced materials. It was possible for them to cast bronze at such a great size, but they were unable to guarantee the finished bell would ring true. As attempt after attempt met with dull, unsuitable chimes, the workmen began to lose heart. On the day before the deadline, the lead craftsman's daughter arrived at the foundry, clad in her best clothes, and asked how the work was coming along. On hearing that the situation was still desperate, she flung herself into the molten bronze. Her anguished father was left clutching nothing but a single slipper, as his daughter sank forever into the agonising hot metal. Her death, however, supposedly brought about a great change in the quality of the bronze, leading to a miraculously clear tone on the huge bell.[11]

Despite such desperate measures undertaken to create the perfect capital, Khubilai did not find Beijing wholly to his liking. He spent the hot summer months away from his new capital, far to the north at his secondary residence in Shangdu, the 'Xanadu' of poetic legend. As for the Yuan dynasty itself, it flourished only briefly. The conquering Mongol vigour was soon vanquished by the temptations of China itself – even as Khubilai proclaimed himself emperor, he was adhering to his own upbringing, which had deliberately favoured a Chinese attitude.

The Yuan dynasty did not last quite as long as the Land of Swallows – Khubilai and his descendants were masters of Beijing for just under a century, from 1271 to 1368. Along with their conquests they inherited the same problems as their predecessors – the usual cycles of famine and plenty, health and plague. The Mongols changed China forever and reunited it after centuries of the North–South divide, but did not last. By the mid 1300s, China was suffering from droughts and plagues that made it seem as if Heaven favoured a new change in the ruler. An unidentified disease decimated the Chinese population in the 1330s, likely to have been the very same Black Death that would follow Mongol armies into distant Europe. The disease or something similar returned in an outbreak that killed millions between 1353 and 1354, exacerbating tensions among the survivors.

From the time of the first outbreak, the Mongol hold on China was slipping. Loyalties wore thin among the Chinese population that still greatly outnumbered their Mongol masters, and combined with superstition about the 'bad omens'. The simple struggle for survival did the rest of the job, leading to outbreaks of rebellion in the early- to mid- 1300s. One of the rebel groups eventually grew to present an effective opposition to the Mongols, and successfully chased the Yuan dynasty rulers out of their 'Khan's City'. As far at the Mongols were concerned, the Yuan dynasty continued for many more centuries, but the extent of its territory did not include China.

China, the 'Khan's City' included, now fell under the leadership of a new dynasty, the ethnically Chinese dynasty of Brightness – the *Ming*. For a brief moment, it seemed as if Beijing would lose its old status, reverting to a peripheral town as the power base in China shifted back south. Instead, Beijing's position was strengthened and reaffirmed, almost by chance, and the city was rebuilt once more – improved beyond all recognition. It was in the Ming dynasty that Beijing's all-important central citadel truly took its modern shape. Building on the start made by the Mongols, the new rulers of Beijing would refine their capital to create one of the most stupendous sights in the world – an entire city designed for the imperial masters, walled off from their subjects behind fortress walls, a centre of power designed, and conceived to be the centre of the world itself, an axis about the entire universe was expected to revolve.

4

The Forbidden City

紫禁城

The best time to visit the Forbidden City is off-season, in the dead of winter, when flurries of snow have chased away the tour groups. On a spring day, the early morning crowds are out in force, whisking briskly around the Centre of the Universe in a couple of hours, so the one- and two-day parties can be hurtling down the road in a bus to see the Great Wall before the evening's duck dinner.

The halls tower above the visitor, on stepped ziggurats of marble and alabaster. Draconic gargoyles spit water into the gutters, and great bronze cauldrons sit before each palace — leftovers from the days when the buildings were mostly wooden, and the eunuchs needed a ready source to extinguish localised fires. The tiles beneath my feet are worn down like the flagstones of the Marco Polo Bridge, but not from centuries of attrition. This damage has been done in mere decades, by millions of tramping feet, as armies of tourists roam the main thoroughfares that were once the sole domain of the imperial household. The flagstones are regularly replaced, as are the palaces themselves, renovated in permanent rotation. Some have glassed facades, permitting views of shadowy interiors stacked with dusty memorabilia of the imperial era. Others have been fitted with turnstile gates, hoping to relieve the visitor of a few more coins for that little bit extra – an exhibition of royal jewellery, perhaps, or some *objets d'art* from a particular reign.

The approach to the Hall of Preserving Harmony, like many other imperial buildings, features twin staircases, separated by a carved alabaster image of dragons twirling through clouds. The strange design is a stirring relic of the imperial era – the space between the staircases is decorated because it would never be walked upon. Instead, the Emperor was borne up the stairs in his litter. He would float above the dragon images in his chair, while his litter-bearers trudged up the steps to either side.

In the shadow of the great halls there are smaller buildings used in the past by government officers. Here, there is a building where the military had their quartermaster. Here is another where young princes received their schooling. A strange design hangs *inside*, not outside the door of a former government office. It shows the green figure of a twin-tailed mermaid, her head crowned with a star. Blocky, alien letters surround the strange design, but I am able to make sense of them: 'S-T-A-R-B-U-C-K-S-C-O-F-F-E-E.'

The generation of warfare that led to the establishment of the Ming dynasty did considerable damage to Khanbalikh. The city had grown so large under the Mongols that it was unable to support itself without a stable country to keep its population fed. With the Grand Canal damaged by floods, silt and neglect, many in Khanbalikh had starved. The city's outlying regions were abandoned during the strife and plague; the old Mongol aristocrats were dead or exiled, and few Chinese seemed willing to seek out a place whose importance rested on now-discredited contacts with the peoples of the north and west. China's focus began to shift southward once more – Nanjing was now the capital, with Kaifeng in the west a subsidiary administrative hub.[1]

Nanjing sat at the centre of rich and fertile plains, on a *real* river that was navigable far upstream – it needed none of the artificial watercourses or unstable supply routes of Khanbalikh. Its situation would allow it to grow much larger, and its location kept the new government closely linked to the loyal south, not the untrustworthy north.

With propagandist zeal and a smidgen of superstition, the old north capital was renamed Beiping, 'Northern Peace', seemingly in the hope that harmony would prevail in the old Mongol heartland. Nor was the newly christened Northern Peace expected to fall into ruins. It was still a regional capital, and soon gained a princely patron whose influence would radically change the city's fortunes.

The first emperor of the Ming had an impressive roster of 26 sons, most of who were appointed as regional governors. Only the eldest was kept close at hand in the new capital; the rest were scattered across the empire and tasked with keeping order in their father's name. The emperor's fourth son was given the northeast as his princedom, adopting the arcane title of Prince of Yan, in honour of the region's ancient Land of Swallows. In the midst of empire-wide rebuilding and reconstruction, the newly arrived prince oversaw radical remodelling in the old Mongol capital.

Initially, he had no interest in restoring the city to its full glory. The canal was left derelict, and many of the old Yuan palaces were pulled down. The imperial city itself was reduced in size, its north wall moved southward, to create a more modest and manageable private area. Many of the old Mongol gardens were retained, but Coal Hill to the north now stood outside the imperial city proper.[2]

Even though Chinese civilisation had supposedly been restored, it was impossible to expect a century of foreign rule to have left no mark. In the case of the Prince of Yan, growing up in a Mongol-ruled society seemed to impart certain expectations about the succession. With the death of his elder brother, the Prince of Yan began to expect that he, and not his young nephew, should be recognised as the rightful heir to the Ming emperor. It was a decidedly Mongol attitude towards the imperial succession, and not one that the emperor was prepared to allow. When he eventually died in 1398, he expressly ordered his many surviving sons to stay away from the enthronement of his heir in Nanjing, for fear that they would attempt a coup.

Despite these admonitions, the Prince of Yan set out for Nanjing anyway, and was only thwarted when threatening military forces blocked his path. He returned, embarrassed, to the north, but the damage was already done. The Prince of Yan and his nephew would fight over the future of the empire in a three-year civil war, which ended with Nanjing in ruins, the nephew nowhere to be found, and the administrative centre of the empire moved back north, to the Prince of Yan's home turf. Beijing had become the capital of all China, and would remain so until the present day, except for a brief period in the twentieth century.

The Prince of Yan, remembered in the dynastic histories as Yongle, the Emperor of Perpetual Happiness, was thus responsible for the rehabilitation of Beijing as an imperial capital, not only through his early reconstruction, but also for even more extensive rebuilding undertaken after his victory. It is said that Yongle stayed in the Beijing region out of a sense of military zeal – the hated Mongols were still at large, and he intended to personally lead the mop up operations against them. But Beijing was also his personal power base, and the place where he was most likely to feel safe. There may have been Mongol enemies to the north, but

Yongle also cannot have placed much trust in his many disgruntled brothers or their exponentially expanding families in the south.

From 1406 to 1420, Beijing was a building site once more; its palaces renovated, its lakes expanded and, the grandeur of its Grand Canal restored. The Emperor of Perpetual Happiness faced strong resistance from his engineers; many regarded the city as a doomed venture. Yongle's own Minister of Works dared to refuse the commission, reminding his ruler that the region was still widely regarded as the Waste of the Bitter Sea, and that the dragons of the area were too powerful to overcome. By 'dragons', the minister is likely to have meant the many unfavourable features of the terrain, but to a casual reader, some of the court documents regarding the reconstruction can often seem as if Yongle was ordering his engineers to do battle with serpents and savage beasts.[3]

The two imperial officers charged with redeveloping Beijing were legendarily at odds. Whether this is historically accurate or mere dramatic licence is unknown, but city folklore maintains that they sulked in separate quarters, each determined to prove the other to be a fool, only to be united in their town planning when both received the same vision – the ghost of a young boy, supposedly the spirit of Nezha himself, demigod of past dynasties, the suicidal multi-limbed child-hero who supposedly rode on fiery wheels and terrorised the local dragons. Nezha instructed each of them to 'copy' his own body. It is, so popular legend claims, this imitation of the eight-armed figure of Nezha that caused Beijing to have its Ming dynasty layout.

Even when one has a Ming dynasty city map, and not a later Qing-, Republican- or Communist-era street plan, the idea that the city is laid out in the shape of a giant god seems ludicrous. Geomancers have attempted lengthy discourses on the meaning of Beijing as a recumbent god, suggesting that a certain gate is an ear of Nezha; a certain pair of wells are his eyes; his feet rest on a pair of temples to the south, or that the space in front of the Gate of Heavenly Peace is his lungs. Even before the modern era, local inhabitants regarded such superstition with mild embarrassment, and not even the *feng shui* masters seemed to take it all that seriously. It is not the image of a god in Beijing's town planning that concerns the Chinese, it is the implication that however the city was designed, a substantial element of its origin lay not in human artifice, but in divine inspiration.[4]

The Ming-era reconstruction of Beijing comes accompanied by many other folktales, from merry anecdotes of supernatural assistance, to macabre tales of the grotesque. Yongle initiated an incentive scheme to encourage outlying provinces to aid the project – a decision which led to legends about the reconstruction of Beijing to spring up far from its actual location. In one case, it was said that the distant mountain of *Shenmu* ('Sacred Trees') gained its name for the speed with which timber from the region had been floated down the Yangtze river, ready for shipment north to Beijing.

Since the Mongols left the city in a hurry, it was not a surprise that they left much of their possessions behind. Stories of Yongle's men pulling down Mongol palaces seem only partly born out from memories of demolition and renovation. Officers of the new regime were also likely to have been on the lookout for buried treasure, squirreled away by the departed dynasty.

Folklore soon intervened, and the simple hunt for concealed bullion took on a legendary status, with stories of a man called the Living God of Wealth, blessed, or rather, cursed with the ability to find buried treasure. According to legend, the Living God of Wealth was an ordinary man with an extraordinary gift – somehow, he was able to simply know where valuable objects could be found. But after years of abuse from greedy bullies, he had taken on a hermit's existence, refusing to profit from his own knowledge, and living as a pauper.

It is likely that the story of a dirty, wretched tramp dragged before Ming officers and ordered to lead them to riches contain within it a more tragic tale – that of a loyal servant of the old regime, abandoned by his former masters and tortured by a new order hungry for monetary gain. Yongle ordered them to beat him until he took them to the treasure, and to beat him all the more if he turned out to be bluffing.

Before long, the bleeding, pleading form of the Living God of Wealth brought his tormenters to a patch of waste ground, and told them to dig. Beneath the surface they found ten secret vaults, containing nearly half a billion *taels* of silver. This, we are told, is the origin of the strangely named Ten Vaults Lake, which formed when the great hole in the ground eventually filled up with water.[5]

But even as the brutality of the takeover crushed and beat down the last remnants of the old regime, the new Ming dynasty began to build new ministries and public works.

Down on what was once the southeast corner of the Mongol wall, the shiny glass towers of the modern embassy area loom above carefully tended grass verges. The area has the icy, corporate elegance of business districts in American cities – the roads are wide, the sidewalks empty but for street sweepers, the lush grasses well tended but only for show. One could almost believe one were in Atlanta, were it not for the great stone building that sits at the corner of two main roads like a medieval castle, its thick walls crenellated to protect archers from attack, its roof dotted with the distinctive silhouettes of astronomical instruments – a giant metal sextant, a quadrant, an altazimuth and an armillary sphere.

The Imperial Observatory was originally set up by Khubilai Khan at a different address, but was moved to its current location at the beginning of the Ming dynasty, during one of the city's greatest periods of renovation. It looks like a fortress because that's what it was – it is one of the last remaining pieces of the old city wall, left intact because of its new function, while other sections were pulled down and moved further out as part of the city's expansion.

Many locals don't know what the building is. Modern slang has truncated its name until it is often dismissed as the 'old observation tower'. One can occasionally find Beijing train spotters on its battlements, peering down at the approach to the nearby railway station. It seems that for many taxi drivers and passers-by, it is these anorakked figures that are the 'observers'.

The historical truth is even more surprising. The Imperial Observatory was a vital part of the Chinese world order. The superstitions of court religion demanded precise calculations for planning auspicious events. The portents had to be precisely right for the dating of a coronation or a royal wedding; government appointments needed to be timed to gain the maximum good fortune. Important decisions and journeys had to be postponed until the precise time that the fates would give them the greatest chance for success. In order to keep tabs on these many factors in the Chinese calendar, the Imperial Observatory was responsible for the planning of almanacs and astronomical tables. At first the imperial astronomers were locals; then, in the time of Khubilai Khan, many were Muslims.

During the later Ming dynasty, the observatory became the site of quarrelling foreign factions, as the Chinese and Arab astronomers fought to discredit new arrivals from Europe. The Jesuits, of course, hoped to convert the Chinese to Christianity, but planned on playing a long game by first making themselves and their scientific knowledge indispensable to the Chinese establishment. The Jesuits had more accurate equipment and modern science than their counterparts, and soon ruled the roost when it came to organising the calendar.

Since the earliest times, when unrest in the Land of Swallows was tracked through the appearances of meteors and comets in the corresponding sector of the sky, the inhabitants of Beijing have believed that the constellations reflect and influence earthly events. But if Beijing were the centre of the world Under Heaven, and Beijing's ruler its paramount being, then the rules of propriety demanded that Beijing's centre had a constellation of its own – a central citadel that represented the very axis about which the universe would turn.

Confucius said: 'Ruling by moral example will make you like the Pole Star, which remains firm in place while the other stars revolve around it.'[6] If heaven were a map of earth, then the centre of the world would need to be an earthly analogue of the pole star itself, which was popularly believed by Chinese stargazers to have a purple tint. For this reason, the private citadel at the centre of Beijing, prohibited to commoners for centuries, was known as the 'Purple Forbidden City'. The universe, it was expected, would turn around it, in harmony and awe.

These days, it is known locally as the 'old palace'. It is a mandatory inclusion for the tourist, somewhat to its detriment, since its sheer size and the weight of its story can over-awe the unprepared visitor. For many foreigners, the Forbidden City soon leads to the common condition of feeling 'templed out'. Its side passages are a maze of anonymous russet walls, its gardens an identikit of intricate but nameless buildings. The greatest service done for the site was by Bernardo Bertolucci, whose 1987 movie *The Last Emperor* helped untold millions of foreigners appreciate the Forbidden City in context.

But this is the place where *The Last Emperor* happened. Not merely the location for the Bertolucci film, but the actual place where 'Henry' Puyi, final Lord of Ten Thousand Years, once terrorised eunuchs by riding on a bicycle. Coal Hill to the north was built by human hands, and was the site of the suicide of the last of the Ming. Within the complex, by the ubiquitous postcard sellers, behind the cash machine, is the place where a terrifying Manchu general turned on the steps to address a crowd, announcing that he would be taking over, against the background of a smouldering palace building.

The Forbidden City was the centrepiece of Ming-era Beijing. Much of what remains today is more recent, from the Ming's Qing usurpers, but even so, the basic design has been retained, a recreation of the ancient idea of the centre of the perfect city, at the centre of the perfect world, presided over by the perfect ruler.

Beyond the walls of the Forbidden City, Ming-era Beijing struggled to live up to the architectural plan. Rivers and lakes unhelpfully broke up some of the straight-line streets. The expansion of the outer walls of the city north, creating a suburb that would have completely surrounded the Forbidden City, was never completed, forcing the idealised urban design to fall a little short of the Yongle Emperor's ambitions.

That old favourite, the family of dragons was soon back in local myth, sneaking into town in human form to suck wells dry. They were defeated at last by the architect Liu Bowen, who successfully arranged for the diversion of the waters from a nearby river. One legend tells of a stone mason working on the Beijing project, who thought he saw the dragons making off with the water and gave chase, only to be lured into a dry river bed just before the floodgates were opened, bringing a fatal torrent crashing down upon him. To hear the story told, it seems suspiciously close to an old tale of a sacrifice to a river god.

But Beijing's water supply remains salty and faintly unpleasant – said to be the dragons' last revenge, hoarding all the good water at the Jade Spring in the hills, and leaving Beijing with nothing but the dregs. For the residents of the imperial citadel, the dragons were thwarted by a daily convoy of carts that rolled into the hills to the Jade Spring, stocked up with fresh water, and then brought it back to the palace. Occasionally, exploratory wells would happen upon better supplies inside the city, and wealthy locals would soon buy up the daily supply, such as in Wangfujing, the 'Well of the Prince', now transformed into Beijing's swishest shopping mall. Geomancers attempted to read some sort of pattern into the occasional discovery of a well, claiming that the sites of good wells in Ming dynasty Beijing followed the shape of a giant centipede, sent to burrow into the earth by a sorcerer who was tired of the bitter taste of Beijing tea.[7]

The unnamed wizard was not the only supernatural assistant. A story about the strangely ornate watchtowers of the Forbidden City claims that Yongle ordered his masons to come up with something distinctive on pain of death, and then left them to it. After three months of deliberation (notably, the same deadline given to Khubilai's bell-makers in Mongol times), the builders were running out of patience and hope, and one of the carpenters went outside to get some air. There, he bumped into an aged pedlar who sold him an elaborate cricket cage. Back in the meeting room, the carpenter showed it to his fellow workers, who marvelled at the construction that somehow used nine beams and a eighteen pillars to create a roof with seventy-two ridges. The builders copied the cricket cage in the construction of the watchtowers, and later folklore suggested that the cricket seller had really been the god of carpenters in disguise.[8]

But much of the folklore about the Forbidden City relates to its outer courts – those parts, such as the watchtowers, that could be glimpsed by the commoners. There is a fascination for the historian in being able to stand in the places that centuries of people could only read about in dynastic chronicles – the inner chambers where empresses watched acrobats, or the well where a concubine was murdered, or committed suicide, depending on which spin one believes. The Forbidden City is a place to be savoured over many visits, coupled with reading and appreciation of the many historical moments it has witnessed. The half-day allotted to so many tour groups seems like a pointless exercise – a baffling parade of names and dates, delivered amid a relentless trudge around big open spaces, and occasional glimpses into dark rooms. One first visits the Forbidden City out of sense of duty. Its true majesty and wondrous history takes a lifetime to appreciate.

Although he is remembered as the architect of Ming Beijing, Yongle did not flourish in his new capital. The paint was barely dry on the new Forbidden City when it became the home to scandal. Beijing might have represented a new start for the Ming dynasty, but despite being far removed from the old capitals in the south, it spontaneously developed troubles of its own.

Southern Chinese beauties, those capricious, wilful creatures that had brought down many an emperor in past centuries, were in short supply in Beijing. But that did not seem to bother Yongle – in fact, his particular fetish seems to have been for foreign girls, particularly Koreans from just over the border, who would have been an exotic change from the women of south China. One such concubine, Lady Quan, died soon after Yongle's return from a campaign, and was later found to have been poisoned by a rival, who had got eunuch attendants to drop arsenic into the poor girl's tea. The matter only came to light several years later as part of palace feud between two other Koreans, when a girl from a poor background accused a snooty palace rival of being the poisoner.

The alleged poisoner was branded and died 'soon afterwards' – an indicator of suicide, enforced or voluntary. The accuser fared little better, since she later hanged herself, afraid that a platonic relationship with a palace eunuch might be regarded as a spiritual betrayal of her imperial master. Yongle, however, refused to believe this explanation, and tortured the dead lady's servants until they 'confessed' that she had killed herself because she was afraid the emperor would discover she was planning to assassinate him.

The allegation led to a savage purge of palace women, with over two thousand eventually implicated and tortured to death. The real truth came out in the dying curse of one of the victims, who revealed that Yongle was impotent. Beijing life had given him terrible rheumatism, and left him unable to carry out his conjugal duties. This had left his many dozens of concubines and wives with perilously little to do, and turned them all upon each other.[9]

With such bad omens, it is perhaps not a surprise that the Chinese began to suspect that their almanacs might be in error. Yongle's successors kept careful tabs on matters of state *feng shui*, questioning and testing many of his city planning decisions. The temple complex to Heaven and Earth he had built in the southern suburbs was radically remodelled. One of its most distinctive buildings, the multi-eaved circular Hall of Prayer for Good Harvests (often simply called the Temple of Heaven today) has become one of the most recognisable buildings in Beijing, although the version that exists today is relatively recent. The Ming dynasty original was struck by lightning and burned to the ground in 1889, although the modern building is supposedly a reasonable facsimile of the original.

After 1534, when Earth-worship was moved to a new, more geomantically appropriate location, the complex was given over entirely to the worship of Heaven, and still has its remarkable circular multi-tiered altar. For many centuries, this was the location of one of the most important ceremonies of the imperial calendar. On the day before the Winter Solstice, the emperors of the Ming and Qing dynasties would leave the Forbidden City in a great procession that nobody would see – the people of Beijing were ordered to remain indoors on pain of death, while the religious procession marched on a road strewn with yellow dust, toward the great Altar of Heaven. The ceremony began before dawn, involving parties of carefully coordinated 'temple dancers' on the lower tiers of the site. The emperor himself, however, was left alone at the pinnacle of the altar, standing before symbolic offerings to the spirits and his ancestors, while his herald read out his prayers, his respects and an annual report of events and accomplishments in the empire. The ceremony would finish with the ceremonial burning of sacrificial offerings, in a series of braziers that flanked the altar, each leading to a great tiled sacrificial oven.

Yongle's workers also radically rebuilt the Mongol walls, which seem to have been largely comprised of rammed earth, and subject to decay and erosion if left untended. The Ming builders faced the earthen ramparts with bricks, or in some cases, built completely new walls within the perimeter of the old ones – the depopulation of the plague period left the former Khan's City not requiring anything near the land area of its heyday.

Wall building also went on outside the city, to legendary effect. The most visible achievement of Yongle's dynasty, begun in his lifetime but not completed until decades later, was the most famous monument of all in China, the Great Wall. The Ming wall was not the first to mark out the northern border of China, but it was a much more enduring undertaking than its prede-cessors. Whereas previous 'great walls', dating back to the time of the First Emperor, had utilised rammed earth, wooden palisades and ditches, the Ming wall was a sturdy bricks-and-mortar affair. Earlier walls had often been used less as border markers, and more as bases from which Chinese troops and colonists could sally forth against the enemies of the north and west. Yongle's wall had a genuine defensive role, with construction commencing in recognition of a new policy towards the Mongols. Unable to hound China's former rulers to a final defeat in their homeland, the Ming dynasty instead hoped to wall them off, out of sight and mind.

Yongle's successors having defined the northern border of China with legendary finality, there were soon Chinese colonists to the north of it. Ironically, it was their relationship with the Manchu people to the north that encouraged the Manchus to consider ruling China for themselves. When the Ming dynasty eventually fell, Chinese colonists from north of the wall, who had gone just native enough to serve new masters, would fill many critical roles in the invading forces.

Today, much of the Great Wall remains in ruins, although several portions have been painstakingly restored to its Ming-era glory. US president Richard Nixon became one of the first high profile foreign visitors to the restored section, infamously proclaiming: 'It sure is a great wall.' In the decades that have followed, the Great Wall has become an industry of its own, and the Badaling section that Nixon saw has become something of a tourist trap. It is close enough to Beijing that a tour bus can take in both Badaling and the Ming tombs in one day, meaning that although the wall is supposedly thousands of miles long, its sections nearest Beijing are crawling with tourists.

Later generations have seen other sections restored, with decisions based largely on either transport access or the opportunity offered for an impressive backdrop. Broken-down sections first attract tourists off the beaten track, then the inevitable hawkers, then the renovators and safety consultants who often strip away much of the historical charm along with the dangers. Today, one must drive for several hours to find a relatively deserted section of the Great Wall, and visitors are encouraged not to – far better, for all concerned, that they are corralled into areas with handrails, public transport access, and a restaurant.

Standing on the Great Wall is a beautiful and terrifying experience. It still has the same effect on modern visitors that it was designed to have on earlier barbarians like the Mongols. Stretching away as far as the eye can see, across mountains and valleys until it peters out on the horizon, only to lurch back into view again as it rings a militarily important site a few miles further over, the Great Wall still sends a message to any who see it. *This is what China can do*, it says. *Not just to you, but to ourselves* – not for nothing did earlier defensive projects gain the wall the nickname of 'the Longest Cemetery'. The Great Wall is a testament to the millions that died to build it, and a symbol of fortress China.

Yongle also laid the earliest foundations of Beijing's tourist industry, by commanding his ministers to come up with a list of peerless attractions that could be promoted as the Eight Great Sights of Beijing. His reasoning was political, aimed not at encouraging vacationing visitors, but at whipping up a sense of local heritage. Yongle still faced unsteady support in the south, and his Eight Great Sights project was designed to encourage poems, songs and prose to establish Beijing's image as a true capital, and hence his own as the rightful ruler. These eight wonders of Beijing, as chronicled in the early Ming dynasty, are a drearily twee collection of half-hearted seasonal slogans, sounding precisely like the kind of nonsense one might get in a new town without many old or famous landmarks, from a committee who could not be bothered to look too far from their office window.[10]

The Marco Polo Bridge, still standing after many centuries, was dragged in as one of the exhibits, notably because it had cropped up in a poem from one of the emperors of the Jin dynasty. What was good enough for the Khitans was good enough for the Ming: the moon at dawn on the Marco Polo Bridge. The Great Wall was also a mandatory inclusion, although the feature chosen was not technically part of the Wall proper, but an isolated fortress on a mountain pass, tarted up with an irrelevant spot of nature promotion to become one of the Eight Sights: the lush greenery around the fortress at Juyong Pass. The committee followed up with the sun on the Golden Terrace (a site that is no longer extant). Seeing a pattern that might do their selection for them, they scrabbled around for more elements and opposites. The trees around the old ruined entrance to the ancient capital, the Thistle Gate – they might do. But since there was already a mention of greenery, the committee added that the sight was only 'great' when the forest was viewed in the mist.

There were pretty rainbows out in the hills; in the mists where the Jade Spring of fresh water bubbled to the surface . . . they heard. Snow looked good on the Western Hills . . . sometimes. In spring, it was often pleasantly warm on Hortensia Island . . . apparently. The ripples on the water, the committee decided, looked nice in Beihai Park. And that was the eight, done – conspicuously with a couple being visible from the same spot, as if someone had dashed off the last two as an afterthought on his way to work.

The desire to keep Beijing as the capital, and to maintain relations with the peoples even further north, risked recreating the old north–south divide. Far to the south, Nanjing was kept as a sleepy alternate-capital, its ministers and officials diligently shadowing the functions of the true centre, just in case Beijing should have to be abandoned. Even as the campaigns against the Mongols petered out, and the Ming mindset became more about hiding behind walls than proactively pursuing new frontiers, the Ming people continued to intermix across the border.

Nanjing, as it would eventually turn out, was not the only place that was shadowing Beijing.

North of the Great Wall, the 'barbarian' people of Manchuria were developing a love, respect and covetousness towards the power and wealth of the Ming dynasty. In their own capital of Mukden, the Manchus began to formulate ministries and behaviours designed to copy and eventually surpass those of the Chinese in Beijing. Eventually, the ruling clan of the Manchus proclaimed a new decree – that the Ming dynasty was fated to fall, and that it was the destiny of the Manchus to replace it. Just as Khubilai Khan had proclaimed the foundation of his Yuan dynasty several years before conquering China, the Manchus proclaimed their own replacement for the Ming somewhat in advance of their actual rule. At first, they called it the Golden dynasty in imitation of the Jurchen rulers of old. But a generation later, when a Manchu army poured across the Great Wall into China, the Manchus had settled on a new name that would be the last of the imperial dynasties to rule China. They called themselves the Qing, the Dynasty of Clarity.

Bust of Lower Cave Man at Zhoukoudian.

Lions on the Marco Polo Bridge.

The Marco Polo Bridge.

Khubilai Khan, statue by
Cheng Yunxian.

A distinctive white pagoda atop Hortensia Island.

The waters of Beihai Park – one of the Eight Great Sights.

Watchtower on the Great Wall at Simatai.

The walls of the Old Observatory with their castle design.

The flood-suppressing Bronze Ox at the Summer Palace.

The emperor's path up to one of the palaces of the Forbidden City.

The Empress Dowager's marble paddle steamer at the Summer Palace.

Right: Portrait of Mao from the Tiananmen gate.

Below: Statues of Chinese revolutionaries from Mao's mausoleum.

Bottom: Tiananmen gate.

People's Liberation Army soldiers on a visit to the Temple of Heaven.

Modern apartment buildings are a new answer to the hutongs.

5

'Peking'

北京

For a moment, I am alone in the chamber. The walls are painted in the bright red of marital bliss. The screen in front of me is painted with a giant pattern comprising conjoined *xi* ('happiness'), a traditional nuptial decoration. This quiet, deserted hall looks much like any other to the average Western visitor, particularly on a day trip to the Forbidden City, where one big bare room in a big red hall can often end up looking very much like another. But there is something special about this place, with its double-happiness on the wall, and the entwined dragon and phoenix designs repeated on the furniture. The lanterns similarly bear a double-*xi* design. This quiet hall, this very room, is a place of bridal celebration. Three different Qing emperors spent their wedding nights here. They drank wine with their new brides on this very bed with their new empresses. There is joy in this room, but also nervousness, and pathos. Of the three emperors, two of them died young in suspicious circumstances, the victims of a palace conspiracy by old widows determined to cling to power. The silence is remarkable, as is the chill – even though it is a warm sunny day outside, I see a cloud of my breath in the air.

The haunting silence is broken by an ear-splitting mechanical shriek – a handheld loud speaker that has a built-in theme tune. At the touch of a button, it blares the first few bars of the *Laurel and Hardy* theme, at a decibel level twice that of the average ice cream van. It is in the hands of an earnest Chinese guide, who has used it to shock a group of Italian tourists into stunned silence.

'THIS IS THE HALL OF EARTHLY TRANQUILITY!' she yells into her megaphone. 'FORMER RESIDENCE OF THE EMPRESSES, AND A PLACE OF SILENT CONTEMPLATION!' As if to underline her point, she triggers another burst of ice-cream-van Laurel and Hardy from her sonic weapon.

Although history books usually show a tidy single date for the regime change, the fall of Beijing to the Manchus in 1644 did not bring the rest of China immediately with it. A resistance movement continued for another generation, until the last rebels either forgot what they were fighting for or faded into organisations indistinguishable from criminal gangs. In an unguarded moment at a banquet, one Manchu nobleman claimed that his people originally had little chance of taking China south of the Yellow River. Instead, they had set their sights on seizing the northern territory once held by the Khitans and Jurchen, but had been startled by the lack of true Ming resistance, and by the numbers of Chinese subjects willing to join their cause.[1] As a result, in the early days of the Qing dynasty, the Manchus did not have much time for rebuilding. The surviving buildings of the old Ming Forbidden City were simply repurposed for the new owners, with little more than a change in signposts and the occasional lick of paint. It took many years before Qing-era buildings began to replace those of the departed dynasty in the centre of Beijing.

It seems churlish, disrespectful even, to point out the greatest irony in the history of fortress China. At the crucial hour, the Great Wall failed – or rather, despite all the sturdy architecture of defence, China fell through human error. At the time of the collapse of the Ming dynasty, there was no money left in imperial coffers to pay the many thousands of soldiers guarding the northern frontier. The general Wu Sangui, charged with holding back the northern barbarians, successfully held his army together with charisma and promises, until the fateful day when he switched sides.

Dwindling finances on the wall were not the only sign of trouble. Rebellions in the hinterland offered still more worries to the fretful Ming dynasty. Even as thousands of Ming soldiers stared north from the battlements of the Great Wall, Beijing fell to a Chinese rebel. Li Zicheng, a former postman, had led a bandit existence for several years before leading his forces to the gates of Beijing itself. The city fell swiftly – its troops demoralised, its cannons without ammunition, it defences compromised by years of neglect and corruption.

The fall of the Ming dynasty created a number of villains for Chinese history, on every side of the conflict. The last Ming emperors were painted as unworthy successors to the noble Chinese who ousted the Mongols, failing their subjects and their ancestors by losing the support of Heaven once more. Wu Sangui is a classically tragic figure in Chinese drama – a soldier torn between his allegiance to a doomed dynasty, temptations on offer from devilish invaders, and a desire for revenge against the usurper who has killed his father and raped his lover. Only Li Zicheng has gained some form of rehabilitation. In the Communist era, he was lionised for his role in toppling the old imperial order, and for attracting humble farmers to his standard. His statue now stands amid the traffic on the road northwest of Beijing, near the off-ramp to the Ming tombs.

The Manchus ruled China during a tumultuous period in which geography no longer kept it out of contact with other powers. But during the Age of Exploration, as the Portuguese and Spanish were rounding Africa and mapping the Americas, the Chinese stayed put. In the earliest days of the Ming dynasty, Chinese embassies sailed as far as Madagascar, but the great age of Chinese exploration was soon brought to an end. Finances dwindled, the Ming emperors had other problems on their minds, and besides, it was thought unseemly that imperial embassies would go in search of recognition of their own greatness from foreigners – far better that the barbarians approach China themselves, with the correct degree of etiquette, and a fair amount of fear and trembling. Beijing itself may have played some part in this – the landlocked capital, forever clinging to its inland canal routes and its camel trains across the plains, may have encouraged a landlubber attitude in its ruling class. Whereas Chinese in the south, in the great river port of Nanjing or the seafaring towns of Fuzhou or Canton had traditions of maritime trade, the northern Chinese preferred to look inwards, at the great sea of grassland that extended to the west, or the parched, dusty deserts of the hinterland.

If anything, the Manchus were even more landlocked than the Ming dynasty. With a nomadic background and a love of horsemanship and the steppe life, the Manchu ruling house was pathologically afraid of the sea. In the seventeenth century, they briefly ordered the complete depopulation of the seacoast to a distance of some thirty miles, hoping to cut China off completely from the undue influence of the coastline. Instead of building a navy, the Manchus briefly attempted to push the sea itself out of sight and out of mind, creating a swathe of barren territory more than a day's march across, patrolled only by government troops with orders to kill any loiterers on sight.[2]

With such an attitude, it is perhaps not surprising that the Manchus were taken by surprise by the arrival of the European nations in the Far East.

Beijing's northern location played a part in China's decline during the eighteenth and nineteenth century. Contact with European powers was initially limited to the far south of the Chinese continent, through the port of Canton. Europeans pushed for further trading opportunities and contacts inland, but Beijing remained largely unimpressed by their requests and entreaties, and unaware of their urgency.

The aging British ambassador George (later Lord) Macartney arrived in China in 1793, hoping to establish diplomatic relations. Instead, he scandalised the Manchu court by refusing to kow-tow before the Qianlong Emperor, and by looking down his nose at a valuable gift of jade. Meanwhile, the Emperor was baffled by Macartney's entreaties; China was the Centre of the World, and prided itself on needing nothing from barbarian neighbours. The concept of 'trade' was entirely beyond the Emperor, who advised Macartney: 'You . . . should simply act in conformity with Our wishes by strengthening your loyalty and swearing perpetual obedience, so as to ensure that your country may share the blessings of peace.'[3]

Macartney left a record of the few days that he spent in Beijing that October, writing that the city was 'one of the largest in the world, and justly to be admired for its walls and gates, the distribution of its quarters, the width and allineation (sic) of its streets, the grandeur of its triumphal arches and the number and magnificence of its palaces.' The city that Macartney saw still bore reminders that the Manchus were conquerors – policing was 'singularly strict', and Macartney was surprised by a curfew that effectively shut down every main street, 'shut up by barricades at each end and a guard . . . constantly patrolling.' He was also taken aback by the population's close-packed living arrangements.

> [A]t Pekin one scarcely meets with any but men, as the women seldom stir abroad. The houses . . . are very closely inhabited, it being no uncommon thing for a dozen people to be crowded into one small chamber that in England would be considered as a scanty accommodation for a single person. . . . None of the streets are paved so that in wet weather they are covered in mud and in dry weather the dust is excessively disagreeable pervading every place and every thing, but what renders it intolerably offensive is the stench.[4]

The city retained the 'chess-board' design of wide thoroughfares as mentioned by Marco Polo, and within each square was a maze of small alleys and tracks. Sectors within each square usually comprised clusters of buildings around a central water well, a *huttog* in Manchu, which gave its name to the Chinese term *hutong*. In the imperial period, the *hutong* residences were often mansions and palaces, but by the twentieth century, they were often subdivided time and again, until several families crammed into a residence once intended for just one.[5]

Although Macartney was careful not to voice his disapproval to his hosts, he might have been surprised to learn that they agreed with him. Like the Mongols, the Manchu emperors did not enjoy Beijing dust either, and preferred to live some fifteen kilometres outside the Forbidden City, in a series of mansions and sculpted gardens near the Jade Spring, known collectively outside China as the Summer Palace.

The title is a misnomer. Although officially intended as a residence for the hot months, the Summer Palace proved irresistible to the emperors for much of the rest of the year – its name falsely implying that the sovereigns were hard at work in the capital for longer than they actually were. They often packed up and headed for the Summer Palace as early as the Chinese New Year in February. At the actual height of summer itself, they were often nowhere near the Summer Palace, but sought even cooler climes many leagues to the north.

Kangxi, the Emperor of Hearty Prosperity, spent as much time at the 'Summer' Palace as his court responsibilities would allow. His son and successor Yongzheng, the Emperor of Harmonious Justice, effectively moved his administration to the gardens, and built extra palaces in its southern quarter so he could run the state without leaving his vacation residence. By the time of Yongzheng's successor, Qianlong, the Emperor of Strong Prosperity, the Summer Palace was arguably more important to the imperial family than Beijing itself.

The Summer Palace's finest garden was later known as the Yuanming Yuan (Garden of Perfect Brightness), the 'Versailles of the Orient', with a large lake, around which were clustered nine connected islets, each representing one of the ducal domains of ancient times. Other landscaped gardens clustered nearby, including the Yihe Yuan (Garden of Nurtured Harmony), set around a former reservoir for old Beijing's crucial water supply, now remodelled as a whimsical recreation of idyllic southern living, as Kunming Lake. Fairytale pagodas, statues, and pavilions were dotted around the lake and in the hills above, creating a false-perspective impression of being deep in the countryside, far away from the bustle of the capital.

A bronze ox, its back carved with a sacred spell to suppress floodwaters, gazes out over the lake, close to the majestic Seventeen Arch Bridge that reaches out to an island in the centre of the lake. The ox's presence reflects climatic troubles elsewhere – floods had heavily damaged the Marco Polo Bridge in 1698. The Emperor of Hearty Prosperity also renamed the river itself, calling it the Eternally Pacified, and hoping thereby to make it behave.

Flooding rivers, droughts and occasional famines were nothing new. But China was entirely unprepared for the arrival of the European powers. Towards the end of the Ming dynasty, European visitors were treated with amusement and condescension in Beijing. By the 1700s, the European community in Beijing was growing. The Russians were the first sizeable group to be new in town, as emissaries of the great European power were able to literally walk all the way east to Siberia, and then south.

As marine technology advanced in great leaps, sea-faring nations were soon following behind, particularly the British. Then, as now, China was recognised as a market with gargantuan potential, ready to be moulded, coerced, even bullied into cooperation.

Lord Macartney's kindly entreaties to the Chinese hid a greater urgency – the balance of trade between the English, who had a thirst for Chinese tea, and the Chinese, who famously claimed that they wanted for nothing. The American Revolution had cut off old trade routes across the Atlantic, and Napoleon was on the rise in Europe. The British took extreme measures by finding a new cargo that they could sell to the Chinese in exchange for tea – opium.

British popular myth, particularly in the old Chinatown of London's Limehouse district, would later suggest that the Chinese were a race of addled dope fiends. Such stories tended to avoid the inner truth, that they were often made so by British salesmen. Opium was grown and harvested in British India, then shipped to south China, where the British became the drug pushers for an entire nation.

The exponential rise in the number of opium addicts in the south was a cause of concern to the Chinese. The government in Beijing tried to ban the sale of opium, and imposed severe punishments on its smugglers and sellers. But such well-intentioned decrees were of little use in the south, where forceful British officials such as Charles (Lord) Napier were agitating to be allowed ever greater trade privileges. The Chinese administrator Lin Zexu wrote a stern letter to Queen Victoria, demanding that she rein in her pushers, but the message never reached the British monarch, who was herself an occasional dabbler in opium. The frustrated Lin eventually seized and burned all the opium in Canton in a heady conflagration in 1839. His bold act was answered with the arrival of a British fleet, brandishing modern cannons that far exceeded anything that the Chinese had to offer. In one of several actions later known as the Opium War, a fleet sailed up the Yangtze and effectively cut the Chinese empire in two, blocking Beijing's tax and trade conduits to the south. China was obliged to concede to the Treaty of Nanjing in 1843, an infamous document that opened certain Chinese ports to British trade, permitted Christian missionaries into the country.

The rest of the nineteenth century saw China enduring successive humiliations at the hands of the European powers, as emissaries arrived from other countries, each determined to grab concessions on the Chinese coast ready to trade in the hinterland. Without a strong military or any means of resisting forces bolstered by the Industrial Revolution which had, until that point, largely passed China by, Beijing lost great swathes of coastal territory to foreign leases. The most famous, kept in foreign hands until the very end of the twentieth century, were Hong Kong (UK) and Macao (Portugal), although China is littered with the evidence of other, forgotten concessions. Shanghai and Tianjin still have handsome boulevards built for urban Europeans, while Qingdao retains a German brewery (Tsing Tao) set up by its European 'guests'.

Equally embarrassing was the imposition of 'extraterritoriality' – the new arrivals treated the Chinese in much the same way as they had already treated the natives of America and Africa. It was decreed that Chinese laws and restrictions did not apply to Europeans – a stinging insult to the world's oldest continuous culture, which was now not even permitted to legally arrest, try or detain foreign criminals on its own territory. The cherry on the cake was the concept of Most Favoured Nation status, wherein any concessions granted to one power would have to also be granted to another. The imperial household in Beijing was no longer the master of its own country, and it was only a matter of time before this led to open unrest. Simple protests over food shortages or local injustice were often magnified along unwelcome political lines – in particular, much of the unrest in mid- to late-nineteenth century China dragged up the old spectre of the Ming dynasty, serving to remind Chinese that even though they were suffering indignities at the hands of foreigners, their own rulers were themselves a clan from outside China. As Manchu power weakened, whispers began that they had lost the support of heaven, becoming all the louder after 1853, when the Yellow River dramatically and disastrously shifted its course so that it flowed south, not north, of the Shandong peninsula, devastating thousands of square kilometres of farmland.

Religious and criminal movements suggested that it was time for a change. Ethnic minorities in isolated areas proclaimed rebellious enclaves that often went unpunished for years, while criminal elements took advantage of bad feeling towards the Manchus to paint their unlawful activities with a brush of Ming restorationism, or even the establishment of a completely new order.

In the south, the first sign was the cataclysmic Taiping Rebellion, more than a decade of violence that some insist on calling the Taiping War, in recognition of the awful damage it did to China – leading to more deaths than even the First World War. Promulgating a bizarre mixture of revolutionary fervour and Christian dogma, the Taipings' leader was precisely the sort of enemy that China's indignity had created. Having failed the civil service entrance exams on several occasions, he woke up one morning and proclaimed that he was the son of God, waving pamphlets that he had picked up from a Christian missionary. His revolutionary movement, attracting the poor and dispossessed to his banner, would later be regarded as a forerunner of Communism, although none of its supposed higher aims were achieved before the Taiping rebels were wiped out, with cataclysmic loss of life.

Much to the embarrassment of the Chinese, the British took over parts of local government during the crisis. Even though Shanghai was in the grip of the Taipings, British customs officials continued to run trade in the area, collecting taxes on behalf of the impotent Chinese government. It was incidents such as this that would later be used to twist the arm of the government in Beijing, stripping it day by day of its powers and responsibilities

With the Russians pushing from the north, the Taipings uncontrollable in the south, and other foreign powers boasting that they could bring China to heel when the imperial household could not, the violence came to Beijing itself. When it did arrive, it did so in the form of European aggression, as the demand for more trade and diplomacy was delivered out of the barrel of a gun. In 1860, a force of some 200 ships and 17,000 Europeans landed at Tianjin in August, and stood before the gates of Beijing before the end of September.

In October 1860, the French and British combined forces marched on the Summer Palace, expecting that the Xianfeng Emperor would be there. He and his entourage had already fled north to Jehol, leaving the new arrivals to wander, quite stunned, through the priceless artefacts of the gardens and palaces. Determined to teach the Chinese a lesson, the Europeans took everything they could carry, smashing whatever was left behind. Many of the priceless objects ended up back in London and Paris in museums. Others were carted off as plunder. Captain Charles Gordon, a young engineer with the British forces, reported that 'after pillaging it, [we] burned the whole place, destroying in a Vandal like manner, most valuable property. . . It was wretchedly demoralizing work for an army. Everybody was wild for plunder.'[6]

Two days later, the British leader Lord Elgin ordered for the gutted buildings of the Yuan Ming Yuan to be burned in reprisal for the deaths of several European prisoners in Chinese custody. A witness, Reverend R.J.L. McGhee wrote:

> Out burst a hundred flames, the smoke obscures the sun, and temples, palaces, buildings and all, hallowed by age, if age can be hallow, and by beauty, if it can make sacred, are swept to destruction. A pang of sorrow seizes upon you. . . No eye will ever gaze on those buildings . . . records of by-gone skill and taste, of which the world contains not the like. You have seen them once and for ever . . . man cannot reproduce them.'[7]

Antiques and plunder from the Summer Palace flowed onto the European market, with bargain hunters snatching up little bits of *chinoiserie*, even as they tutted at the behaviour of the French and English.

The burning of the Summer Palace was yet one more sign of the end of the empire. The Xianfeng Emperor, nominal ruler of China, died aged just 30, leaving an infant child as his successor. Meanwhile, the new emperor's regents reluctantly agreed to the ultimate insult – the presence of foreign legation buildings in Beijing itself, in a 'Legation Quarter' just to the south of the Forbidden City. Beijing, and China itself came to be regarded by the foreign powers in much the way that they regarded its six-year-old Tongzhi Emperor, as an ineffectual child that needed to have its responsibilities shouldered by others until it was able to fend for itself.

The word 'Peking', which means nothing to the Chinese, carries within it at least part of the story of the foreign guests. When Lord Macartney came to China in 1793, he recorded the name of China's capital in his journal as 'Pekin'. Thomas Wade, a former ambassador who ended his days as Cambridge's first professor of Chinese, published the first English-language textbook of Chinese in 1867. Wade developed a syllabary for romanising Chinese sounds during his long career in the diplomatic service, encompassing large amounts of time far to the south in Hong Kong, where the local dialect was much harsher and more guttural. The word *Beijing* was hence written in Wade's syllabary as *Peking*. He expected the P to be pronounced as a B, and the

K to be pronounced as J. To actually make the sound 'Peking' with Wade's syllabary, a linguist would need to add the apostrophe-like voice markers and write it *p'e k'ing*.

Needless to say, this spelling, particularly as codified later on by Herbert Giles to form the Wade-Giles system, has eternally confused the non-specialist as to Chinese pronunciations. Matters were not helped by variation in pronunciation within China itself. Down in the south, where so many British visitors were concentrated in Hong Kong, the local language pronounced Beijing as something more like Bakging, which actually made the Wade-Giles rendering make more sense than it ought to. The confusion would continue for half the twentieth century, until Communist China, determined to free itself from the shackles of imperialist influences, even in the writing of its own language, approved the creation of its own romanisation system in 1958. The new system, which writes Beijing as 'Beijing', was not officially introduced until 1979, hence explaining the common discrepancy between generations. I grew up hearing the word Beijing, reinforced when I began studying Chinese under teachers from Mainland China. My parents' generation grew up hearing 'Peking', and many of them have yet to shake it off.[8]

Regardless of the activities of the foreigners, it is often said that China's worst enemy in the latter half of the nineteenth century was a young widow of the departed Xianfeng Emperor, who would serve in various capacities as a regent for her son and then her nephew. Her most common name today is Cixi, but she is ofter known by the title that she initially received as the mother of Xianfeng's successor – the Empress Dowager.

Only 26 years old at the time of her husband's death, the Empress Dowager would dominate Chinese politics for the next 40 years. Then as now, it is the Empress Dowager, a cosseted concubine turned *grande dame*, who is most often held responsible for the spectacular demise of imperial China. This is, perhaps, unfair. Chinese folklore speaks of an ancient curse, that predicted a woman of her clan would destroy the empire, but it seems overly simplistic to blame a 26-year-old woman for China's failure to hold off foreign predators and domestic revolution. In the early years of her reign, the Empress Dowager had more pressing matters at hand – forced to share the power of the regency with noblemen administrators and the late emperor's chief wife. Cixi was only a concubine, and received a position in the hierarchy solely for being the mother of the new emperor. Cixi may have been pig-headed, but she was a creation of centuries of stultifying tradition. She was barely literate – an extant edict in her own handwriting botches many characters – and wholly ignorant of the challenges that China would face if it were to square up to foreign pressure.

In 1872, her son came of age, supposedly bringing an end to the regency. But the reign of this Tongzhi Emperor lasted a mere three years, as he embarked on a series of ill-advised schemes, including a cripplingly expensive attempt to repair the Summer Palace, and the demotion of many of administrators who had annoyed him during the regency. Dead, allegedly of syphilis, by 1875, the Tongzhi Emperor left no heir of his own, prompting Cixi to adopt her three-year-old nephew, proclaim a new regency, and thereby buy herself another generation in power.

Cixi famously used money earmarked for the modernisation of the Imperial Navy to renovate her holiday homes at the Summer Palace. The shoreline of Kunming Lake still has the most notorious of the results – a marble terrace in the shape of a stylised paddle steamer, constructed at the Empress Dowager's order to give her another idyllic spot for moonlight banquets. It is an intricate, beautiful folly in every sense of the word, and an enduring monument to Cixi's blinkered grasp of reality, a fortune squandered on an playful garden ornament at a time when China's military struggled to hold off ironclad foreign warships with antique wooden galleons.

It is easy to laugh at Cixi's silly frivolity, but it can be argued that the renovation of the Summer Palace was not a bitch-queen's bid for luxury at all, but a desperate attempt by some of her officials to get her out of the way. For decades, factions in the Forbidden City sought to lure Cixi out of power with the one tool available to them – the good life. In one famous incident, palace officials waited until Cixi has expressly ordered that she not be disturbed during an opera performance, before taking advantage of the strict order to pass and carry out an order of execution against one of Cixi's cronies. Similarly, we might suppose that administrators hoped to lure her out of Beijing, a day's ride away in the Summer Palace, so that others might be able to get on with the business of running the country. Whether these men would have done a better job of holding off disaster, we will never know; their ruses never quite worked, and Cixi remained in charge.

No new ships were bought for the Chinese navy after 1888, leading to a humiliating defeat in the Sino-Japanese War of 1894–5, when Japanese incursion into Korea was met with brave but futile Chinese military intervention. Even as the Manchus clung to past glories, and hired officials on the basis of their family connections or mastery of classical texts, modern achievements in engineering and technology were changing the face of the globe. Beneath the notice of the Manchus, the history of north China was fast becoming tied to the fortunes of the railway that the Russians had built right across Eurasia. With the establishment of Vladivostok on the Pacific, a name that ominously translates as 'Domination of the East', the Russian Empire could now move men and *materiel* swiftly to and from the Pacific. The Chinese had little say in the movement of Russian trains both around and through the Manchurian homeland of the imperial family; instead, the nearby island of

Japan offered the strongest resistance. Seeing themselves as the 'British of Asia', the Japanese desired to be seen as equals of the Western imperialists – which, for them, meant swiftly modernising and then demanding similar concessions in China to those received by the Europeans.

Meanwhile, the Foreign Legations took over an entire city sector, to the east of Tiananmen, the Gate of Heavenly Peace – perilously close to the Forbidden City itself. Their ideas came with them – a railway from Tianjin edged into the city by 1896, and a pitiful few of Chinese and Manchu court officials attempted some reforms to strengthen China. They did so in the name of her charge, the Guangxu Emperor, leading the Empress Dowager to effectively dismiss him – although still nominally the Son of Heaven, he was kept sequestered in a palace while his supporters were rounded up and executed.

Beyond the walls of the Forbidden City, there was a rift across China between the small ruling class of Manchus, and the great masses of ethnic Chinese. Running low on friends, the Manchus fatally offered tacit support to one of the few uprisings that aimed to oust 'foreigners' without including the Manchus in their number. This was the Boxer Rebellion. After further signs of Heaven's displeasure – flooding in 1898, then droughts in 1899 and 1900 – a society calling itself the Righteous and Harmonious Fist (*Yihe Quan*) rose up, supposedly to defend Chinese tradition from unwelcome foreign influences.

Made famous by innumerable movies in the ensuing century, these 'Boxers' preached a form of martial art that purported to make its adherents invulnerable to bullets. Although this was soon proved to be untrue, the Boxer movement grew in stature, until armies of anti-foreign militia roamed China in search of missionaries and merchants to murder.

They reached Beijing in June 1900, at first in small groups, easily marked out by their red headbands and belts. By 8 June, the embassy district was worried enough at rising reports of attacks on foreigners in Beijing to request permission for more soldiers to be brought up from Tianjin for their own protection. On 11 June, the Boxers struck close to home, murdering a Japanese diplomat, ahead of a mass Boxer invasion two days later.

The first Boxer assault on the Legations was repelled with a few gunshots. The following week, one of the Empress Dowager's wilier officials leaked a forged document that claimed that the foreigners had demanded the right to take over all administration in China. The angry Boxers were back in the thousands, trapping the foreigners and their families in the Legation Quarter in an armed siege that lasted for several weeks.

The siege of the Foreign Legations achieved worldwide infamy, uniting newspapers in Europe, America and Japan in their horror of the way foreigners were treated in China. It was an offence to the tender sensibilities of the Christian world, which regarded the activities of missionaries in China as sacrosanct, and the foreign media was soon rife with stories of brave soldiers fighting off sword-waving Boxer rebels, and devout missionary matrons cowering before rapacious rebels.

It was not until the 14th August that a relief force arrived in the city, with Russians, British and Japanese racing for the chance to be the first on the scene. In fact, it was a Sikh soldier with the British army who was the first into the besieged area, crawling through the filthy sewer gate and along a ditch to announce the arrival of rescuers to the surviving residents. Chinese residents of Beijing had fled in their thousands, fearing the foreigners even more than the marauding Boxers. Cixi herself, disguised in peasant clothes, had been one of the anonymous figures in the retreating throng, abandoning the city from which her clan supposedly ruled the world.

While the relief of the Legations was a feel-good story all over the western world, the incident spelled disaster for Beijing and its surroundings. The city was partitioned between the rescuing forces, which imposed harsh military order on any Chinese who had not already fled the city. Beijing became divided under stern American-British-Japanese martial law for the following year, while the occupiers refused to negotiate with the Manchus until the Empress Dowager herself returned from hiding. Most Favoured Nation status even extended to plunder – German troops arrived late for the fighting, but still received a sector of the city.

The ensuing weeks saw Beijing torn apart by its new owners. Boxers had broken into the Summer Palace, under renovation after the Europeans' earlier looting, and raided the new buildings for timber. The multinational expedition force sent to deal with the Boxers also descended upon the Summer Palace, snatching any remaining statues or stone carvings. Back in town, entrepreneurs wrenched the famous astronomical instruments from the roof of the Old Observatory and sent them to Germany, where they stayed for more than a decade, until the Germans were obliged to give them back in the aftermath of the First World War.

The Empress Dowager did not return with her court until January 1902, arriving by train in what could have been a symbolic gesture of defeat. Instead, her arrival seems to have been regarded with elation by many of the Europeans present. When she offered them a little bow as she passed, they burst into applause. A similar selective amnesia about her involvement in anti-foreigner movements seemed to carry over into the settlement over the incident, which left the Empress Dowager herself largely unaffected, although several of her officials were forced to take responsibility for the sequence of events, and paid with their lives.

But it was too late. The Manchus would never recover from the Boxer Rebellion. Russian incursions into the northwest, originally undertaken in the name of restoring order, were slow to retreat, leading eventually to the Russo-

Japanese War of 1904–5 that saw Japan victorious and the Czar's authority fatally undermined. Reluctantly, the Manchus began preparations to modernise in the Japanese style, sending a delegation to the West to learn its ways, although conservative opposition was still so strong that a suicide bomber attacked the delegates as they prepared to leave Beijing.

The Guangxu Emperor, still in seclusion, and the Empress Dowager both died in 1908, on days so close to each other that foul play has long been suspected. They were succeeded by another powerless infant, who screamed and wailed at his coronation, until his father tried to soothe him with the fateful words: 'Don't worry, this will soon be over.' The boy's reign title was announced as Xuantong, or Proclamation, perhaps implying a hope that China would soon be reformed by a series of imperial fiats. But he is better known today as 'Henry' Puyi, the Last Emperor.

6

Northern Peace

北平

Revolution had been brewing for decades, nurtured by overseas communities of Chinese, by secret societies that claimed to have been laying in wait since the fall of the Ming dynasty, and encouraged by democratic movements abroad. When revolution came to China, it came to the fractious south. Beijing, power centre for the old order, was slow to fall into step with the times, and often fell behind.

Although still supposedly the Ruler of All Under Heaven, by 1912 the Last Emperor ruled only within the Forbidden City. Beijing itself was under the control of Yuan Shikai, an aging military man who had been called out of retirement in an attempt to keep order in the city. Yuan still had an army, and offered such an implacable resistance to the revolutionaries in the south that they were often obliged to play along with him. Although one Sun Yatsen is remembered as the first president of republican China, he was in power only for a matter of days before he resigned his post in favour of Yuan Shikai.

China hovered on the brink of fragmentation, as several provinces toyed with the notion of proclaiming their own independence. But while the notion of democracy and republicanism was strong in some places, in Beijing it seemed possible that the fall of the Manchus would merely lead to a new imperial dynasty. Yuan Shikai was declared president for a five-year term, soon extended to ten, and by 1915 he began preparations to become an even more powerful head of state.

It had been more than a decade since the last sacrificial rites were performed at the Altar of Heaven. Yuan Shikai eventually agreed to perform the rites himself, in what was either a half-hearted attempt to appease religious conservatives, or more likely a failed bid to establish himself as the new emperor.

Many critics paint Yuan Shikai as a corrupt official intent on becoming a new emperor – and in fact he may well have been – but it is worth noting that many citizens of the new China almost expected it. China had seen many dynasties come and go, and it would not have been the first time that a warlord had marched into Beijing, toppled the incumbent dynasty and then proclaimed his own. Republican, Nationalist rhetoric, with all its talk of democracy, may not trickled down to the man in the street, particularly when the concept appeared so foreign.

It is only now, a century after the event, that we know the Qing dynasty to have truly fallen.

In 1912, many would have still expected, or hoped, or dreaded that some form of restoration might occur, either in full or in some sort of compromise that offered the Last Emperor a form of constitutional monarchy.

Yuan Shikai's government ordered that the Great Qing Gate, opposite Tiananmen, the Gate of Heavenly Peace, should be renamed the Great China Gate, removing the tablet on its eaves that associated the name of the edifice with that of the departed dynasty. But workmen were scrupulously careful as they removed its sign, deciding that it would be unwise to destroy the 'Great Qing' sign, since there was no way of telling at that moment whether the dynasty was truly over. Hedging their bets, they decided to wrap it carefully against knocks and scrapes, and to stow it out of harm's way in the gate's attic, ready for a swift, Orwellian reversal of nomenclature in the event of a sudden restoration. As they stashed the sign in a suitably undisturbed corner, they found another tablet of similar size and shape, obscured beneath centuries of dust and grime. The writing on it read 'Great Ming' – it had been stashed in a similar fashion in the seventeenth century by their predecessors.[1]

The end of the First World War saw massive celebrations in Beijing, as thousands paraded past the Tiananmen gate. It was widely believed that the defeat of Germany would see the restoration of Shandong to China, and with it, one might presume, the removal of any need for the British to hang on to Weihaiwei, or for other foreign powers to keep up their bases on other parts of Chinese soil. The mood of the times, at least, suggested that the foreigners would now begin their retreat from China, with the return of Shandong as the first of many. However, many of the partygoers in the Beijing streets were unaware that Shandong had already been sold out by their government, who had offered the province as security on a 20 million yen loan from Japan. When the subject of Shandong came up at the Paris Peace Conference, the Chinese were scandalised to hear that the German territory would be 'restored' not to China, but to the Japanese who currently occupied it.

Protests broke out over both the loan itself and the perceived betrayal of Chinese interests; celebrants in front of the Tiananmen gate were replaced with student demonstrators. Whipped into a frenzy, they turned east towards the old Legation Quarter, where they planned on attacking the Japanese embassy. Armed guards presented too imposing a threat to the crowds, so they turned towards a new target. Instead of lynching the Japanese ambassador, they attacked the house of the Chinese Minister of Communications, whom they rightly suspected had been a prime broker in the Shandong scandal.

The fact that a paltry number of guards were able to frighten them away from the Japanese embassy speaks volumes. Although there were thousands of demonstrators, the number of active militants was considerably fewer – at first, only thirty-two arrests were made. Regardless, news of the incident spread throughout China and found support in many other cities. In Beijing itself, it was followed by strikes and a boycott of Japanese goods. Although the initial troublemakers had already been released, further demonstrations seemed much more wide-ranging – there were three thousand arrests, until the prisons of Beijing were overflowing. In June, Chinese diplomats in Europe refused to sign the Treaty of Versailles.

This uprising, on 4 May 1919, became enshrined in later annals as a crucial moment in the history of Chinese Communism. It was, so the Party historians later decreed, a moment when the Chinese people had had enough, and turned on the government toadies who had betrayed their trust. The fact that the protest happened in front of the Gate of Heavenly Peace, in the area we know better today as Tiananmen Square, was to make later Chinese governments incredibly jumpy at the sight of student protestors in the same place. The 4 May Incident was a landmark in the history of Beijing and the history of China, but for some it also set a dangerous precedent. Seventy years later, a government that regarded itself as the legitimate inheritor of the 4 May spirit would send tanks into Tiananmen Square to avert a similar event.

The 4 May uprising established student radicals as prime influences on decision-making, and brought the authority of the republican government into disrepute. It is no coincidence that a Communist youth group was founded in Beijing by 1920.

Meanwhile, Beijing lost its status as capital. The shaky republican state in the south proclaimed that Nanjing, the South Capital, was the new centre of the Chinese government. Beijing, perilously close to Russian and Japanese interests and the Manchurian heartland, had fallen out of fashion, and was renamed, with a degree of blind faith, Beiping, or Northern Peace.

The years that followed saw the city buffeted by the interests of local warlords, resurgent republicans and Japanese intrigues. Manchuria itself, homeland of the Qing dynasty, fell under Japanese control, and became a puppet regime ruled by the Last Emperor – he might have lost China, but he clung to Manchuria for a while longer.

In 1937, trouble broke out over a seemingly minor incident at the Marco Polo Bridge, when Japanese officers demanded to be let into a fortified town nearby to search for a missing one of their company. When Chinese soldiers inside the town refused, the Japanese advanced across the bridge with tanks on 8 July. Chinese forces retook the bridge the day after and later agreed tentative terms with the Japanese, in which the soldiers agreed not to advance further. Despite this, Japanese tanks were in Beijing by 29 July – supposedly to defend the interests of Japanese businessmen and residents.

Northwest China had become a Japanese vassal, and the second 'Sino-Japanese' War had begun. Although it started as a conflict between Japanese occupiers and Nationalist Chinese defenders, in Beijing and other occupied zones, mainly along the coast, the war would escalate until 1941, when the Japanese attack on Pearl Harbor brought the Allied forces into the conflict on the side of the Chinese.

Beijing antiquities suffered a predictable degree of neglect during the period. With no imperial family left to even consider repairing the Summer Palace, the ruins fell even further into disrepair, raided for building materials by desperate locals, and even gaining a small cluster of shantytowns. Nor would the end of the Sino-Japanese War, subsumed within the Second World War since 1941, lead to reconstruction for Northern Peace. The Japanese might have left, but the city was still in a dilapidated state, and suffered all the more when a new conflict broke out. The Chinese Communists, who had worked under a fragile treaty with the Chinese Nationalists during the Japanese occupation, now turned on their former allies.

The Communists enjoyed strong support in the countryside, where local peasants often remembered comparatively few sightings of Nationalists during the campaigns against the Japanese. Before long, the civil war saw the Nationalists chased out of China, retreating to the offshore island of Taiwan, which retains a Nationalist (i.e. non-Communist) Chinese government to this day.

The supposed 'Northern Peace' came to an end in October 1949, when Chairman Mao stood at the balcony of the Tiananmen gate and proclaimed that 'The Chinese people, comprising one quarter of humanity, have now stood up.'[2] He spoke to a crowd who had seen the worst of China's civil war. Tellingly, their various hurrahs still bore the taint of the imperial age, wishing Mao 'ten thousand years' as if he were a new emperor. Modern propaganda carefully rewrites the sense of it – the huge words on the gate today co-opt the idea for all, and not a single person. 'Ten thousand years to the great unity of the world's peoples,' they say, before the line is broken by a massive portrait of Mao. The line continues on the other side: 'Ten thousand years to the People's Republic of China.'

Never quite self-sufficient, Beijing had been cruelly tortured by the disruption of its food supply from the Nationalist south. Shortages had taken their toll in the closing days of the war, while money had been rendered meaningless by inflation at 8000 percent. The nominal restoration of its status as a capital had meant nothing under Japanese occupation. It did not become fashionable to call the city 'Beijing' again until 1949, and the city had been marginalised during a crucial two decades of technological development. A handful of main thoroughfares had been paved and smeared with rudimentary tarmac, but they had long since crumbled beneath years of neglect, the heavy rumble of military vehicles, and the inevitable consequences of Beijing's icy winters. The rest of the town was changed little from the days of the

Boxers – more than two thirds of the residents still drew their water from wells, and few homes had electricity. The previous winter, people had been literally dying in the Beijing streets, with sweepers reporting 200 fatally frozen or starved in a single district. Those who made it to January 1949 were forced to endure a series of purges, as the victorious Communists hunted down thousands of Nationalist sympathisers and deserters in the city.

With old money only available in ludicrously high denominations, or bearing the unwelcome faces of pre-Revolution rulers, traders were forbidden to use anything but the new Communist notes. More pragmatic residents turned to barter or the black market, and money itself fell out of fashion. Some form of rationing, either of certain basic foodstuffs or certain cloth, remained in force for another thirty years.

The surviving palaces of the Manchu era were transformed into homes and offices for the Party faithful. Mao himself took up residence in the luxurious Zhongnan pleasure park to the west of the Forbidden City. But Mao and his associates had arrived in Beijing after years of deprivation as guerrillas in the wilderness. They had lived lives of relative austerity – even when able to put down roots in their Yan'an headquarters, they were essentially living in caves. Since many, including Mao himself, came from peasant backgrounds to begin with, they brought a new and radically uncomplicated attitude towards Beijing. Beijing in the early days of the

Communist era still retained vestiges of its imperial grandeur; enough for Soviet advisers in the 1950s to develop a reputation as shopaholics and bargain hunters. But Mao would soon put a stop to that.

Much of China's imperial treasure had already been spirited away to safety by the fleeing Nationalists, at first stored in vaults by the government-in-exile at Chongqing. After the war, the treasures were relocated to Taiwan, where they remain today in one of the five most richly appointed museums in the world. Their continued presence there remains a matter of Chinese diplomatic embarrassment, comparable to a similar argument of preservation and ownership to be heard between Britain and Greece over the Elgin Marbles. The chief difference is in the rhetoric – the governments in Taipei and Beijing both claim to be the rulers of China, and hence the most appropriate guardians of the antiquities. To this day, many priceless relics of Beijing's history are hundreds of miles away in the National Palace Museum in Taipei, the subject of recurring quarrels between the rival governments.

Mao's grand scheme for Beijing was like his grand scheme for China itself, a state of permanent revolution, deliberately defying tradition. The most noticeable casualty was the city wall. At first, the damage was minor. Taking a leaf from the foreign railway builders of the nineteenth century, the town planners of Beijing smashed wide gaps in the old wall to allow better transport access. In the age of intercontinental ballistic missiles, there seemed little point in having such a small barrier to the outside world. The worst damage would come in the 1960s, when a China drunk on modernism decided to do away entirely with the walls of the Manchu city. They were pulled down to make space for a combined ring road and subway. Those pre-Communist buildings that survive in Beijing are lucky to have done so after years of warfare and a Soviet-inspired remodelling.

Tradition itself was a dirty word – *tradition* meant centuries of imperial despotism, the suppression of the workers, the enslavement of women. Particularly strong in the early 1950s, when things were still friendly with Soviet Russia, was the desire to emulate Soviet modernism. This is most clear of all in Tiananmen Square itself, deliberately designed as a rival to Red Square in Moscow, and dominated by the giant column of the Monument to the People's Martyrs.

Following Soviet Russia's example, China under Mao threw itself into vast, strenuous national initiatives, beginning with the First Five-Year Plan. Many Beijing buildings were pulled down and replaced with brutalist state architecture, but nothing quite so brutal as the troubles that would follow among the Chinese themselves. Merely because the Nationalist Chinese were gone, it did not follow that all was well. The Korean War plunged China back into a conflict on its doorstep, while the Nationalist regime in Taiwan continued to boast and brag that it would soon return to take China back from the Communists.

There was argument within the ranks of the Communists themselves – some supported the Soviet Russian model; others argued that there were unique conditions in China that required a uniquely Chinese solution. Further confusion broke out when it was revealed that the Russians themselves were in disagreement. In 1956, Nikita Khrushchev scandalised the Communist world by denouncing the late Josef Stalin, on whose personality cult Mao had modelled his own. It led Mao to invite denunciations of his own in his Hundred Flowers campaign to encourage criticism of Communist progress, only to turn on his critics with the purges that followed.

The Second Five Year Plan saw ten great architectural projects put in place to mark the tenth anniversary of the founding of the People's Republic, including the Great Hall of the People that dominates the western side of Tiananmen Square. But despite being the capital again and serving as a home to the Party leadership, Beijing lagged far behind many other towns in terms of its production.

In an attempt to stave off the droughts and water shortages that had been a perennial feature of Beijing life from the time of the legendary dragons, the Communist leadership decided to build a new dam up near the tombs of the Ming emperors. Massive public 'voluntary' labour ensured that the dam was completed within six months, although it would appear that Communist engineers relied more on blind faith than they may have been prepared to admit. Once complete, the dam created a reservoir that is still rarely full – nobody had dared point out that many of the rivers flowing into it were dry for much of the year. Such pointless, gigantic but fruitless projects became a feature of the early Communist era – with much wasted effort, wasted time and wasted lives.

Another project, the Miyun Reservoir, had greater success, taming two rivers that were often prone to flooding, and creating a new water supply for Beijing. But even the Miyun was not trouble-free – much of the early work was almost washed away during rainstorms in 1959, and early plans to use excess water to create a navigable canal were abandoned.

The Summer Palace began a slow process of restoration – Kunming Lake returning to its former function as a staging post for aqueducts into Beijing proper, while the surrounding area was reinvented as a public park. The ruins of the European assaults were left as they were, allowing Party faithful to reflect upon the implications of a weak China and foreign aggression.

The worst excesses of Mao's era came at its close, when a generation of children raised on the thoughts of Chairman Mao reached their rebellious teens and turned, in his name, on the Party itself. The Cultural Revolution, spearheaded by the fanatical Red Guards, sought to destroy much of what was left of old China. Many of those museums, temples and artefacts that had not been irreparably damaged in a century of unrest were destroyed in 1966. If it were not for the intercession of Premier Zhou Enlai, the Forbidden City and Beihai Park might also have been ruined by the Red Guards.

Nobody would deny that putting hungry peasants in charge of *objets d'art* was bound to end in disaster, but there were other factors. Maoism's inventor was a man out of time, a peasant boy made good, undoubtedly bright, who studied hard to gain a Confucian education, only to discover that he had been born in an era where his classical knowledge was next to useless in an age of railways and power stations. He spent the rest of his life making up for it, refusing to admit that newfangled knowledge required more than willpower to master. His country origins and his classical reading often gave his pronouncements a sort of homespun quality to his audiences. To intellectuals, he could come across as pig-headed, ignorant or chillingly facetious. But to the masses, he sounded like a plain-spoken man of the people, always ready with words of managerial encouragement, always on hand with a few blindly optimistic parables of the utopia to come. When running a guerrilla campaign in the wilderness, it was enough to inspire his troops on to victory. It was, however, no way to run a country. Blithe dismissal of scientific reality was less of an issue when there were no engines to start or combine harvesters to service. But similar denials of bad harvests and poor production were to plunge China into a secret famine that killed millions in the early days of Communism.

Far from creating enduring edifices and artefacts to benefit the people, Mao's era often created little more than empty spaces – gaps where buildings should have been, the absence of joy and freedom, shortages of food and other necessities, a lost generation of doctors and engineers, exiled to the countryside to 'learn' from the peasants, and thousands upon thousands of people quietly made to disappear.

7

Empty Spaces

Initially, I thought it would be a journey just like any other. I had been photographing the observatory in the east of the city, and hailed a cab just outside the last remnant of the old city wall, by the newly restored watchtower. But when I asked the driver to take me to the Underground City, he suddenly lost the ability to understand me. I drew him the Chinese characters. He shook his head, and all but kicked me out of his cab.

The next driver was a similar case. Initially, he was so eager to snap up a rich foreign fare that he swerved across two lanes to get to me. But once I told him I wanted to go to the Underground City, he blinked blankly and said he had no idea what I was talking about. I pointed it out to him on the map, but he acted as if it wasn't there. Eventually, we reached a compromise; I named the corner of a street that was near the entrance to the Underground City. With some reluctance, fully aware that I would be heading off in search of a place he had sworn did not exist, he swung his car around and drove me there.

He dumped me without ceremony in a swish business district, and pulled away with a screech of tyres. I walked away from the wide road into a tiny side alley, where the glass-sided buildings gave way to the patchy tiles and single-storey huts of a typical *hutong*. Melon-sellers pretended not to see me, and a tea vendor suddenly developed a great interest in his shoelaces. A mother grabbed two children close to her and scurried indoors, and I began to feel like the bad guy in a spaghetti western. Eventually, I found what I was looking for – a simple doorway in the street, flanked by a couple of small stone lions. I gingerly poked my head around the frame, and came face to face with a young woman in army fatigues, who all but spat her noodles out in surprise.

'Hello,' I said. 'Can I see the Underground City?'

She looked around herself in panic, and called downstairs for reinforcements.

'How did you find us?' she asked, setting down her noodles and standing almost to attention.

'There is,' I pointed out timidly, 'a sign outside in two languages.'

Two more women in camouflage arrived, and immediately began interrogating me. Their questions were not the snarling demands of the average Chinese customs official, but polite queries delivered with an icy smile. How did I find them? Where exactly had I come from. How had I even heard of the Underground City? When I demonstrated that their secret base had half a page to itself in the Lonely Planet guidebook, they seemed faintly crestfallen.

The first stirrings of the Underground City were humble enough – bomb shelters sunk into basements all across the city, at the height of Cold War fears of nuclear Armageddon. The emperors might be gone, but it only took the faintest whiff of paranoia in Chairman Mao for the whole city to be engaged with pick and shovels. Before long, news had drifted in from the Soviet Union of grander schemes – entire towns constructed inside mountains, designed to hold fast against atomic weapons.

Those first basement shelters were extended out and down by tens of thousands of conscripted workers, carved by hand. Two stories beneath the streets, human labour scraped spaces in the rock for a hospital, a cinema and a military arsenal. Although scraps of archive footage show the shelters cluttered and crowded, with residents growing mushrooms and raising chickens in apocalyptic squalor, today the tunnels are white and bare. An occasional portrait of Mao or Cultural Revolution slogan adds a scrap of local colour, and antechambers behind half-hearted partitions still seem full of material like a Cold War jumble sale. My guide, a short, chirpy girl in camo-pattern clothes, accompanied me 'for my own safety', pointing out lesser tunnels devoid of electric light, and helping me across places where flooding forced us to balance on precarious duckboards. She was friendly enough, but something about her demeanour made me neglect to mention I learned my Mandarin in Taiwan.

There is a romance to the Underground City, in the bizarre way that it is presented to the outside world. Thousands of Beijing residents formed the work gangs that carved out the tunnels. They dug in fear for their very lives, not just from foreign atomic weaponry, but also from their own leaders, who swore them to the utmost secrecy. This stealthy attitude persists today – the Underground City is a well-known tourist attraction among foreigners, but kept menacingly quiet by Beijing locals, who are discouraged from visiting themselves. As for those like me who brave the obstacles, a theme park Cold War experience arrives – traditional Chinese inquisitiveness, which can often strike the Westerner as plain nosy, takes on an exotic, exciting sheen when doled out by girls dressed as soldiers.

But that is part of its charm. The Underground City is a creation of innuendo – unmentioned and denied, allowed to flourish in the imagination. Rumours cling to it like weeds. Wide-eyed visitors whisper that its tunnels extend for hundreds of miles beneath the city, that it forms an empty space beneath the ground like a negative Great Wall. Guides repeatedly emphasise that it stretches across 85 square kilometres, with at least one arm reaching out all the way to Beijing airport, and another to the port city of Tianjin. Some visitors report finding signposts at underground crossroads, pointing to distant Nanjing, but surely these are merely jokes or hoaxes?

Those few Chinese who are prepared to discuss it at all fall victims to their own country's media blackout. None are completely sure when it was built – it makes more sense for it to have been constructed in the 1950s or 1960s, but most seem convinced that it was dug in the 1970s. What little has been written about the Underground City highlights Russia's 'Brezhnev Doctrine', which threatened to invade any Communist country that did not adhere to a very Russian concept of Communism.

China and the Soviet Union had long been drifting apart, but disagreements over the nature of Communism were no longer matters for mere debate. Back in Moscow, Leonid Brezhnev made it clear that he was prepared to defend Moscow's brand of Communism by invading Communist states that dissented. Czechoslovakia and Hungary served as small but ominous examples. Beijing and Moscow risked turning into full-blown enemies. Chinese and Soviet troops clashed in 1969 over the border island of Zhenbao, and the septuagenarian Chairman Mao feared, with some justification, that open conflict might break out.[1]

Except that is not quite true. The Zhenbao border skirmish was provoked by Mao himself, in one of several attempts to show the United

States that he was no friend of the Soviet Union.[2] At the time that many would have us believe that the tunnels were under construction, America was well and truly on a path to becoming China's friend. The only American invaders in Beijing were a startled team of ping-pong players, caught up in diplomatic intrigues when one innocently suggested it might be nice to see China, and swiftly whisked away on a surprise tourist attack. When the coast was declared clear, it was Richard Nixon who made the greatest gesture of all, descending upon China for a historic meeting that helped lure China back into the international community. Surely, it was no time to be digging tunnels?

Were they even dug at all? The section on view to the public is impressive, but we only have the guides' word that it stretches across the entire city. They would say that, wouldn't they? Like the caves of Zhoukoudian, like the stones of the Great Wall, it is not the dank passageway itself that impresses, but the thought of thousands more like it, lacing the Olympic city in Cold War stealth. But I have not seen a map of all the tunnels. Nobody has. Could it be that the Underground City is not a physical feature at all, but an ideological one – a frightening vision of a state that will stop at nothing to preserve itself? Not for nothing, the bulk of the visitors that come to the Underground City are overseas Chinese – excitable tourists from a Taiwan still viewed by Beijing as a rogue state, ready to hear outrageous war stories about the Communist war machine. They come to be amazed by the fanaticism of their one-time enemies. And then they buy a skirt.

Its largest room, a meeting hall ten metres below street level, has been leased to a Jiangxi silk company. Just when one's day cannot get any more surreal, one is surprised by a lecture on silkworm cultivation and invited to take part in the picking and preparation of silk from cocoons. It is an enlightening lecture, and all the more strange for taking place in a secret bunker.

But what if the Underground City is real? How many Beijing banks have vaults that lie precariously close to a tunnel network? How many apartment blocks have foundations undermined by secret dwellings for forgotten Party cadres? One need merely look at the Great Wall to see what China is capable of. Why *not* dig a city beneath the earth? Perhaps there is another reason for the Underground City's stealthy status – the government prefers not to reveal just how big it is. Or perhaps much of it has already been repurposed. Just as Londoners in the Blitz used the Tube as a bomb shelter, perhaps Beijing refashioned much of its underground network for use by subway trains. It is, perhaps, not a coincidence, that whispered secrets about family members conscripted to dig an 'Underground City' appear to coincide precisely with the construction of China's first subway in 1969.

Opening in 1971, the Beijing subway was only one of many modern developments that heralded China's slow emergence from the hell of the

Cultural Revolution. International flights returned in the early 1970s, along with telegraph and phone links to the outside world. A generation of angst at the United Nations was ended when the People's Republic of China took over the Chinese seat on the Security Council. The Nationalist Chinese on Taiwan were now diplomatic orphans, recognised by ever fewer other states, losing their friends one by one, and forced to come up with increasingly intricate ways of describing themselves as independent without saying the word. It was not until the early 1980s that China itself was prepared to declare the Cultural Revolution a mistake, and its instigators traitors.

Lord Macartney may have once expressed surprise at the close-quarter living arrangements of Old Beijing, but the Communist era saw residents packed even closer. Old Manchu mansions, outbuildings arranged around a central courtyard, were brutally repurposed to hold five, six seven or more families. For much of the twentieth century, Beijing's *hutong* neighbourhoods became synonymous with socialist squalor – the central wells of old replaced with single toilet facilities to serve all the surrounding buildings. Already forced into each other's laps by the small living quarters, Beijing residents were required to share what we might also optimistically call a 'bathroom' with a over a dozen strangers.

Some, however, are more equal than others. The Party is still a major presence in Beijing.

Turn north of Tiananmen Square, and walk the long straight road to the west of the Forbidden City, and the streets are hauntingly deserted. There are none of the traditional amenities – no roadside hawkers, photo stores, bistros or convenience stores. There are no beggars, no grannies selling postcards. Nobody is loitering, because anyone who does is moved swiftly along by the military police. This is where the political faithful live, as they did in Mao's day, clustered around the Zhongnan Park.

China might remain a one-party state, but there is still discord (some might say debate) within the Party. A state that owed so much of its origins to the 4 May movement could not easily end all public protests, particularly when Communism was supposedly founded on the will of the people. Late in 1978, the first stirrings of protest were felt again at what became known as the Democracy Wall – an innocuous section of sports stadium brickwork, that became a magnet for posters and poems outlining things that needed to be done. Before long, the Democracy Wall was relocated to a nearby park by government order, and later protestors were obliged to have their comments screened by the authorities first.

Other protests showed unsettling signs of the rebellions of the past. The city erupted in violence in May 1985, when the home team lost a soccer match against Hong Kong, and thousands of hooligans poured out to vent their anger, somewhat ironically, against 'foreigners'.

The unrest was met with a swift and tough crackdown on the offenders, and a hurried government apology:

> Last night's incident is the worst of its kind in the history of sports in the People's Republic, and the most damaging to China's international image. This type of ignorant and brutish behaviour is quite out of keeping with the stature of our capital city.[3]

The year 1989 saw the most famous political protest in modern Beijing, a chilling reminder to the outside world. It began, supposedly with the death of Hu Yaobang, a relatively liberal politician who had been forced to resign over contemporary student protests, and died soon after of natural causes. Some of his student supporters were soon in Tiananmen Square to show their support, and were joined by older members of the workforce, unhappy with recent price hikes. The Tiananmen Square protests thus already began in confusion, with disaffected Chinese assembling in the square and demanding . . . *something*, although it seems difficult to see what. *Democracy* seems to have been the buzzword – although the first stirrings of a free market was precisely what was causing the price hikes that had so angered some of the protesters in the first place.

Whatever this democracy was, it soon gained a new icon, courtesy of students at the Central Academy of Fine Arts, who assembled the famous Goddess of Democracy in just four days, a ten-metre statue of Styrofoam and papier-mâché, supported on a metal frame. Its size was carefully calculated for extreme visibility, since decades of propaganda had made the students amateur experts – if the army smashed down the statue, as they eventually did, it would be a powerful political statement in its own right. Until that moment, the Goddess was carefully placed in the square facing the giant image of Mao himself on the Gate of Heavenly Peace, defiantly brandishing a flaming torch in a manner that drew inevitable comparisons with the Statue of Liberty in New York.

By May 1989, there were hundreds of protesters camped out in Tiananmen Square, and all attempts to move them had failed. Sympathetic government officials had pleaded with them not to make a spectacle, with voices that became all the more strident as several hundred protesters resolved to go on hunger strike. Levels of government embarrassment climbed steadily as the date approached for a state visit by the Soviet leader Mikhail Gorbachev. Keen to avoid an encounter between a Russian reformer and student radicals, the Chinese government routed Gorbachev's motorcade through a series of outrageous detours to avoid Beijing's main thoroughfare.

With Gorbachev's departure, the gloves were off. At 10:30pm on 3 June, the People's Liberation Army was sent in to clear the square. The use of the military to police a civilian disturbance ended in tragedy, an event remembered today as the Tiananmen Square Massacre. Protestors were forcibly removed from the square and from their enclave to the west of it – which would have placed them right outside the Party residences in Zhongnan Park.

Precise details, however, are hard to come by. Those like myself, who watched the whole thing on television, were initially led to believe that thousands of people had died. These numbers seem based upon vague guesses supplied by harassed medical personnel and shocked foreign reporters at the scene, and may have confused casualties with fatalities. Not that a single death was justified, but in the years since the massacre, it has been difficult to find a list of the dead that climbs above two hundred. The trauma of the Tiananmen Massacre had far reaching effects. Liberals like Zhao Ziyang were drummed out of office, blamed for the very unrest that he had tried to dissuade. Martial law stayed in force until 1990, and might have been upheld for longer if it were not for Beijing's desire to normalise its appearance to the outside world. The economic reforms that some protestors demanded more of, and others wanted to stop for good, were briefly delayed in the aftermath, but soon reinstated in China's inexorable drive towards a freer market. In the years since the PLA smashed the fragile Goddess of Democracy into pieces, much stronger, more enduring replicas of the statue have sprung up in overseas Chinese communities – most notably on the western seaboard of North America, where they continue to stir controversy between supporters and opponents of the Communist regime.

In the hours leading up to the attack, there was a debate among the protestors as to how they should meet it. Many were keen to leave the square peacefully, although as on 4 May seventy years earlier, a militant element was determined to fight back. To hear the army's version of events, it was these militants, armed with petrol bombs, who fought back against the PLA. There were military casualties, too, in the Tiananmen Square massacre, eliciting considerably less sympathy from the international community.

One soldier was faced with an intense diplomatic situation when the path of his tank was blocked by a lone figure. The unidentified man clutching two carrier bags, who faced down an entire tank column, became Beijing's most famous resident. In an iconic moment of twentieth century, the unknown rebel harangued the driver of the lead tank about his mission, until passers-by wisely dragged him out of harm's way. His precise identity and his ultimate fate remain one of the mysteries of Beijing history.

Just a minute's walk from the site of the fateful tank confrontation, Mao's Mausoleum stands where once was the Great Ming Gate, then renamed the Great Qing Gate, then the Great China Gate, the supposed site of several dynasties worth of timid sign-hangers. The body of the old Chairman, or what's left of it, lies in state in a squat building that unkind critics have likened to a 1970s gymnasium. Party faithful queue for the chance to march briskly past the desiccated remains, before browsing the gift shop for some Mao-memorabilia. A lighter, perhaps, that plays *The East is Red*, or a watch that marks the seconds with a waving Chairman.

Mao himself falls in and out of fashion. The current Party line regards him as a necessary evil – a leader that dragged China up by its bootstraps, only to come unstuck when the war was done and the time for peaceful progress arrived. On his deathbed, he offered dire warnings about the future of Communism, reminding his successors that they would have to stick to their guns for the next generation, lest the achievements of Communism be undermined by the temptations of the Capitalist free market.

Twelve years after tanks rolled across Tiananmen Square, the International Olympic Committee announced that Beijing would become the centre of the world once more. In August 2008, the city would play host to the Olympic Games.

8

8:08:08 8/08/08

On the east side of Tiananmen Square, outside the stocky, chunky architecture of the Museum of the Revolution, a digital clock counts down the days, minutes and seconds to the opening of the Olympic Games. Even in scientific, secular Beijing, there is an element of superstition – the number eight is said to bring good fortune and completeness, hence the date and time to which the clock continually ticks away. The Olympics will begin at precisely eight seconds past the eighth minute of the eighth hour, on the eighth day of the eighth month, 2008. As far as lucky numbers go, it has to be the most promising of all.

On the south side of the Square there is a row of tacky trinket shops and bargain clothes stores. Tanned Uighur street pedlars call out to passers-by, hoping to interest them in sticky almond confectionary from Inner Mongolia. A tiny, crippled girl sits on the pavement and carefully scrawls Chinese characters on the stone with a piece of yellow chalk. Her single crutch is by her side, along with a bottle of tea for the long day ahead. She does not look up at visitors or the crowd she inevitably attracts. Instead, she continues her careful work, etching long passages of text on the ground, a battered old paint can at her side stuffed with a few pennies and low-denomination notes from well wishers. Every five lines or so, a cigarette butt suggests that she has taken a break for a hit of tobacco. Her writing is exquisite, her fate, heart-breaking. She is there every day.

Close by are tourist traps of marginally higher class than most – largely offering fake antiques instead of fake watches. The street has been thoroughly pedestrianised, and not even cyclists dare interfere. Boutiques to either side sell cheap artworks, seals carved while you wait, books and clothes. As ever, I poke through the Mao-era propaganda prints, hoping to find something thoroughly unpleasant, preferably a picture calling for the visiting of terrible doom upon capitalist running dogs.

Sensing trade, an old, bearded beggar gets right in my face. He keeps miming that he is hungry, although from the smell of him he hasn't had any trouble finding something to drink. The picture-seller tries to shoo him away, unaware that I can understand what he is saying.

'Get lost,' says the vendor, 'I'm trying to run a business here.'

'Hey,' says the tramp. 'I just want to bug the foreigner.'

'Let him buy something,' says the vendor. 'Then you can bug him all you like.'

Beijing's involvement with the Olympics is surprisingly recent. China only participated in the games on four occasions before 1956, the period of the first Five Year Plan, and had been totally absent thereafter until 1984. The era of the Cultural Revolution killed more than just education and development; it even killed sport.

The achievement of actually hosting the games was thus an incredible learning curve – a superhuman effort, all the more daunting considering the low ebb of international opinion in the wake of the Tiananmen Massacre. Planning began in February 1999, when President Jiang Zemin addressed a national conference in Beijing on 'Promoting the World's Understanding of China.' The President's inaugural speech emphasised the need to 'teach the world' about China; amid suggestions that China might also have something to learn from the world, he urged his people to educate the rest of the world about China's own history. It was an abrupt reversal of the Mao-era obsession with the end of history and the Communist moment. During the Cultural Revolution, China's baby-faced Red Guards had turned on their country's tradition with all the bitter destructiveness of resentful, ignorant teenagers – ill-mannered, vindictive thugs given firearms and a sense of the moral high ground. But Jiang, as the voice of the government, now recognised that China needed to place its twentieth century upheavals in context. For a generation or more, Beijing, and by association, the rest of China, had only showed up in international news as a city of terror and pomposity – the stuffy, totalitarian abode of Party flunkies, the place where tanks were used to put down student demonstrations. The early twentieth century saw China seizing the opportunity to hold international events and conferences, on subjects from women's issues to architecture, slowly training up its hospitality workers for a new form of industry – the service industry.

Beijing hosted the Asian Games in 1990, pouring US$300 million into new building programmes for the expected guests. Some of the initiatives were more cosmetic – the plastering over of bullet holes at the edges of Tiananmen Square, and the repaving of avenues to remove the telltale tank tracks gouged in the road.[1]

Even so, China would not be forgiven so easily. Representatives of the International Olympic Committee (IOC) arrived in 1993 to discuss Beijing's bid to host the Olympics in 2000, where they were regaled with snazzy documentaries about China's rich cultural heritage, and the bizarre promise by Beijing's mayor that all the delegates would be immortalised in a plaque on the Great Wall, if they only agreed. Ironically, part of the Chinese pitch for the games rested on totalitarian guarantees of an obedient population, assuring the IOC that there would be no protests or trouble. In a strange reversal of the drab Mao era, schoolchildren were instructed to dress in brightly coloured clothes, and bussed in to Tiananmen Square by the thousand. Meanwhile, behind the scenes, coal-burning heaters and smoky factories were shut down for the duration of the IOC's visit – in order to ensure clear blue skies over the city, many citizens were deprived of hot water and sent home from industrial jobs.

The Beijing 2000 bid was an impressive effort, all the more remarkable considering how swiftly the Chinese had to learn to play the international game. But Beijing's cosmopolitan status was still doubtful, with relatively few international flights, and a population lacking in competent English skills. The smog-busting ruse had also failed – the delegates thought that environmental protection in Beijing was still substandard. Crucially for a global sporting event that relied on the attention of the world, Beijing's telecommunications were deemed not up to global standards.

Yet none of these problems was a deal-breaker – there was still a chance that the Beijing bid might be successful, if the organisers were able to give the appropriate assurances. According to one rumour, the final straw, tipping the decision in favour of Sydney by just two votes, was an ill-advised moment of old-school Party bluster, when a Chinese official suggested that China would not bother with future Olympic games if it failed to win the 2000 bid. It was exactly the wrong thing to say to the IOC. The Olympics' own mission statement emphasised international understanding, global cooperation, and competition in friendly rivalry; it was not about to cave into retaliatory threats or pre-emptive sulking.

The failure of the 2000 bid clearly hurt the Beijing committee, who had accomplished amazing things, even if ultimately unsuccessful. In the aftermath, Beijing temporarily retreated in on itself, announcing a Five Year Plan of renewal and renovation, which improved conditions in the city for the fiftieth anniversary celebration of the founding of the People's Republic – an aim that would please the Party faithful without the loss of face that a second bid on the international stage might have occasioned.

Crucially, the city's government finally admitted in February 1998 that Beijing suffered from some of the worst air pollution in the world, with the dusty winds from the western deserts augmented by coal-based pollution and the usual smog of an industrial centre with a growing population of automobiles. New traffic laws denuded the streets of some of the worst smoke-belching vehicles, but also bafflingly reducing the number of bicycle-only lanes in what had once been a city where pedals and the pedicab were the default form of transportation.

Beijing residents were encouraged to change not just their city, but also themselves, in a programme to teach them better manners – less spitting in the street, (punished, Singapore style, by a US$6 fine), improved hygiene, and a better sense of personal space. The 11th of each month in the year proceeding the Olympics became 'Queuing Day', in which locals could receive awards for displaying a more internationally acceptably grasp of the importance of standing in an orderly line and not cutting in.[2] A nine-point pledge appeared on billboards all over the city, demanding that 'civilised residents' abide by maxims of acceptable behaviour. Some, such as an admonition to practise family planning, were old-school Chinese Communist slogans. Others, such as the commandment to 'love science and respect teachers' were powerful about-faces from Mao-era contempt for learning. Still more, such as a demand to 'be polite to guests', seemed aimed at preparing Beijing citizenry for an influx of thousands of Olympic visitors. A unit of 'English police' was formed – in fact two scholars, one Chinese and one English, tasked with hunting down bad spelling and grammar in Beijing signs, in order to avoid embarrassing howlers.

Beijing citizens were expected to learn English, with local workers encouraged to take lessons, and useful phrases cropping up in new sections of newspapers. In particular, Beijing taxi drivers were singled out as the likely front line of many foreign visitors' interactions with China, since it was widely understood that foreigners would leap upon the chance to be chauffeur-driven around town for an average cost of US$2 a trip. Beijing cab drivers must hand out numbered receipts, and most appear to have been well drilled in putting the customer first. In my experience, on those rare occasions where Beijing cabbies has got lost or been misdirected (it doesn't help, for example, that there are two Jianguo hotels in Beijing, and locals don't like being told by a foreigner that they are heading for the wrong one), they have stoically refused payment, and have to have their fee all but forced on them. There are still chisellers. I once took a cab from the Summer Palace to the centre of town, and was gouged for a shocking US$16 by the chatty lady driver. She had plainly rigged her meter, but although the trip cost twice what it should, I was still ferried in comfort for less than a dollar a mile.

One of the most severe casualties of Beijing's remodelling has been the old *hutong* lifestyle. A temporary measure that long since outgrew its usefulness, the conversion of nineteenth century homes into twentieth century slums was no longer desirable, not merely for matters of hygiene and living standards, but for simple economies of space. *Hutong* buildings rarely climbed above a single storey, whereas modern China favoured huge tower blocks, which still stacked residents on top of one another, but not quite so literally. More reforms were part of the 'Toilet Revolution', as Beijing locals were instructed in suitable behaviour in toilets. Decades of *hutong* life had left Beijing residents with little sense of privacy, and many foreign visitors return with shocking horror stories of dirty holes in the ground, and communal shit-pits. China gained its own ideal toilet exhibition, designed to introduce the no-nonsense locals to the concept of closing a stall door, or indeed the existence of stall doors in the first place, and, in fact, stalls.[3]

The government also began hunting down Beijing's growing underclass of illegal migrants, comprising peasants and vagrants from other parts of China, lured to the capital by capitalist-inspired dreams of finding their fortune, and often left to subsist in shanty towns, slums and overpopulated flophouses. In September 1999, just one month before the fiftieth anniversary of the People's Republic, officials initiated a purge of the 'Three Withouts': those without papers, those without residence permits, and those without legitimate and permanent income. Thousands of beggars and tramps were rounded up, while a separate modernisation programme demolished 2.6 million square metres of 'illegal structures' – lean-tos, huts and sheds used as accommodation by the rural poor. A common symbol on Beijing walls in the period was the character *chai* – a hand holding an axe – marking any building for destruction, an empty space in waiting. In a moment of foolhardy architectural protest, some new buildings, constructed as part of the renewal protest, also gained a *chai* graffito, scrawled on their walls by unknown parties who disapproved of the speed and nature of change.

The area around the Forbidden City was beautified with a wrecking ball, with the demolition of hundreds of Qing dynasty mansions, now dilapidated by decades of communal occupation. Further out of the centre, officials disbanded and discouraged street markets, leading to a brief but telling citywide shortage of fresh fruit and vegetables. There was also a minor controversy over the demolition of Xinjiang Alley – a street near the university that had achieved a gourmet reputation with ex-pats and students for its *halal* Uighur cuisine. Despite grumblings from foreigners in Beijing, Xinjiang Alley was wiped off the face of the earth in February 1999 – many of the establishments had been illegally built on public land, and hence stood little chance of resisting the demolition order.

Despite the controversies over the approach of the fiftieth anniversary celebrations, they also served to prove how foreign attention could lead to local reforms for the better. The upheavals were unwelcome, even when undertaken in the name of Communism and not the Olympics, but also led to government initiatives to sweeten the pill with 'good news' programmes. Seemingly in an attempt to counter-balance complaints, the people in the rest of China were told that social security payouts were to be increased, and civil servants would receive a 30 per cent pay-rise, backdated for several months. But to many outside observers, the 1999 anniversary celebrations were another Communist sham, with the obligatory military pageant, and counter-productive security measures that forced people who lived on the route of the parade to keep their windows shuttered throughout.

In February 2001, Beijing was prepared to try again to impress the IOC, with the arrival of an inspection team to see how the city had developed. To local residents, it was a repeat of the previous attempt, with a mass mobilisation of street-sweepers and painters before the IOC's arrival, and a round up of the usual suspects. This time, the plan worked, and the IOC announced on 13 July 2001 that the Olympics in 2008 would take place in Beijing.

At least for the tourists' sake, modern Beijing seems keen to forget parts of the twentieth century. Allusions to Beijing's most remote past can be seen in the ultra-modern symbols of its newest event. The logo for the Beijing Olympics is drawn in the style of ancient 'seal-script' – the purview of soothsayers' oracle bones and monuments from the days of the kings of old.

The city has not one but five Olympic mascots, in what the Olympic adverts claim to be a 'message of friendship and peace,' but which really seem to be an acknowledgement of the only force more powerful than *realpolitik* – marketing. The cartoonish Olympic mascots are a menagerie of Chinese creatures, conceived as 'collectable' for all those capitalist visitors, whose children should pester them to bring back not one cuddly toy, or action figure, or key chain, but five. The mascots are a colour-coded team of five; traditionalists might hope to link them to the Chinese elements, but their conception owes more to branded Japanese team-shows like the *Mighty Morphin' Power Rangers*, their nominal leader a fiery personification of the Olympic flame. Foreign visitors can collect the entire set as if they are Pokémon or some other consumerist craze, from the ubiquitous panda and the predictable fish (for water sports) to a politically sensitive Tibetan antelope. But it is the fifth mascot character that speaks the greatest volumes. She is a spirit of the air, appearing on logos for such pursuits as badminton and fencing. As a bird-totem, she is a Swallow, personification of the ancient Land of Swallows, and a symbol of Beijing's long-term poetic association with the birds.

There are, remarkably, still swallows to be seen in Beijing's smog-laden sky. The Beijing Olympic Committee's website devoted an entire section of its website to environmental issues, announcing tree-planting campaigns, high-tech pollution monitors, and improvements in local water quality. The Shougang Steel company, one of the worst polluters in the city, announced that it would reduce its production levels to approximately 50 per cent of former levels for the duration of the games. Seemingly presenting a compromise that was less drastic that the all-out stop of the inspections era, Shougang did not so much reduce Beijing operations as relocate them to another plant. Shougang would continue to belch smoke into the air, but 225 kilometres to the southeast, in Caofeidian.[4]

Beijing is ready for the Olympics – prepared in a way that compares favourably with the advance planning of Seoul, Sydney, and Athens. Tour guides have spent years in training, rotated first from low-intensity sites to ever more lucrative venues, learning their trade as they brush up their English. How many London tour guides, one wonders, will be speaking Mandarin in 2012? But opponents continue to cite continued abuses of power in the name of Beijing's Olympics – the repression of the Falun Gong religious cult, the policing of cyberspace, and a crackdown against Tibetan separatists. The pressure organisation Reporters Sans Frontières went so far as to compare the Beijing Olympics to those in Berlin in 1936, and suggested that far from encouraging the expansion of freedoms in modern China, the Games would only serve to glorify an oppressive regime in the way that 1936 had glorified the Nazis. There are those in the international community who call for athletes to boycott Beijing as many did for Moscow in 1980, lodging an informal protest against the IOC's support of Communist China. Crucially, however, the 1980 Moscow boycott had the backing of the United States, whereas China has enjoyed special attention from America ever since Richard Nixon's historic visit.[5]

But the Olympics are no stranger to controversy, and the selection of Beijing, when considered in Olympic history, is not so out of the ordinary. The feel-good internationalism of the Olympic movement naturally favours the happy memories of past events, and does not dwell on its flipside. There were demonstrations in Mexico before the 1968 games, at which soldiers killed hundreds of protestors, and yet the games went on. There was a military coup in South Korea shortly before the games were awarded to Seoul, and yet the very fact that the eyes of the world would be on Seoul in 1988 was a vital catalyst in achieving important democratic reforms and the effective end of the military regime in 1987. And as Chinese Communist propagandists were quick to mention, nobody stopped the games from going ahead in Atlanta in 1996, despite the ruthless suppression of the Branch Davidian sect in Waco, Texas some three years earlier.[6]

The Olympics are a programme of renovation for Beijing, equivalent to the sweeping reforms of Khubilai Khan and the Yongle Emperor. Every nation that holds the Olympics ends up asking itself the same question. Are we really helping our own people? Will this really improve our infrastructure? Or will there be hungry beggars in ten years, huddling for shelter in the shell of an empty stadium? Beijing has seen many Five Year Plans and grand schemes; it has been razed to the ground on numerous occasions. Will this latest project bring true good, or will it create more discord than it quells, instilling the local poor with grand expectations, and a grand sense of entitlement to something that the future may not be able to provide?

There is still poverty. Not everyone drives in a limousine or works in information technology. As the tourist reaches the final approach to the Great Wall at Simatai, a crowd of hawkers wait hungrily to sell him postcards and guidebooks. With little to do but wait at the top of a mountain, the hawkers have engineered a pecking order based on the time they reach their pitch, and have seemingly have agreed to assign one tourist each. Each group of visitors hence acquires a symmetrical platoon of men and women clutching weather-beaten satchels, earnestly trying to sell the standard accoutrements of hawkers all over China – postcards, dog-eared guidebooks, and Republican-era silver dollars with authentic dirt. Beggars have not so much been banished by the Olympics as rebranded. A beggar with a packet of postcards is officially a beggar no longer, although he can be just as persistent.

'We are farmer,' they say in broken English, pointing at the fields far below. 'This: tower,' pointing at the nearest battlement. In the logic of Chinese etiquette, this makes them guides and you their grateful employer. They do not take kindly to being told that you do not need their assistance, as by the time they find this out, they have already lost their place in the queue on the ridge, and must wait for their next turn.

Not all are as infuriating as the hawkers of Simatai. One swiftly becomes used to the excitable rush of fan-sellers outside the hotels, eager to crowd around any white face. A polite no thank you and they disperse, for now, but for the historian who can place such dispossession and desperation in context, there are still chilling presentiments of the deprivation that led to the Boxers and the Taipings.

Merely because Beijing is now part of the twenty-first century world, it still has its ghosts – or more accurately, immigrant ghosts from other parts of China. Folktales and rumours no longer spread from tavern to tavern, co-opted into musical acts and storyteller routines. Instead they leap across the Internet and television. Beijing children terrify each other with tales of a haunted bus stop, where a disembodied voice calls out to the unwary, asking them the time. Damnation awaits anyone who is foolish enough to answer without turning around – it is the modern equivalent of the black-cloaked murderer of Beihai Park, but the story, like many modern Beijing residents, is not a native. Instead, it has entered local folklore from Hong Kong, where it first appeared.

Beijing is the Cinderella figure, left in the shadows, never before invited to the capitalist ball. Hong Kong is the brassy, loud, ugly sister, the one that got all the attention and all the money, suddenly swanning back home after a century of foreign suitors, dripping with glitz and glamour and high-tech trinkets. In the twenty-first century, Beijing is reinventing itself as a class act – the place with all the history and the monuments, the place where the emperors lived, the place where the government is, and not forgetting the Eight Sights. But while Beijing might have the ruins of the Old Summer Palace, and the memory of its destruction, but Hong Kong has a full-sized replica of the Summer Palace in its heyday – an ongoing argument of style versus substance.[8]

With Tiananmen still an international embarrassment, the Chinese government embarked on a series of initiatives designed to present a different side of Beijing – just as the Emperor of Perpetual Happiness had tried to fake historical continuity with his Eight Great Sights, the People's Republic pushed for the reinvention of many Beijing landmarks. Paramount among these was the grounds of the New Summer Palace, its renovation speeded up, redefined as a site of historical pilgrimage. The ruins of the Old Summer Palace, however, were left in their dilapidated state.

Every now and then, an antique stolen in the sack of the Summer Palace comes on the international market. On the most recent occasion, China was forced to buy back what was rightfully its own, at a London auction house, at a cost of millions of dollars. A debate has raged for decades about the ideal manner to deal with the Old Summer Palace, with some officials arguing for the construction of a replica of its glory days, while others push for the original ruins as a far more evocative and moving sight. When one talks of tourists in Beijing, one is often talking of European tourists, and there is strong and persuasive case for confronting such visitors with the ruins of their states' earlier military interventions.[9]

You cannot buy a model of the Goddess of Democracy in Tiananmen Square. There is a brisk trade at Mao's Mausoleum in tacky Communist-era memorabilia, although it is unclear how many hawkers realise (or care) that many are buying Chairman Mao watches and musical lighters for their own amusement, and not out of any awe for the Party's great hero. Real Communist-era treasures, such as the delicate propaganda posters that once hectored the faithful to Respect the Party and Destroy the Capitalists, are much harder to come by – their very fragility helping their value on the foreign market. But Beijing in the Olympic age would really rather prefer that the foreign tourists stayed away from the socialist era. Sites and opportunities are certainly available to detail the achievements of Communism – particularly the military museum in the west of town, occupying several floors of a forbidding Soviet-era power station, and detailing the various injustices visited upon China by foreign powers. But the Communist era itself, with its headlines of grain harvests and tractor designs, is something of an off-colour joke, amusing in a dreary way for a while, until the poverty, persecution and purges of the Cultural Revolution stifle the smiles.

Upon seeing that I genuinely do have an interest in Mao-era propaganda, an antiques seller shyly proffers a small stack of crumbling posters. Her face goes as red as the East when I happen upon a slogan calling for the collapse of America.

'Times back then,' she says, 'were *interesting.*'

The great halls and staircases of the Forbidden City; the soaring towers of the Great Wall and the statuesque beauty of the Ming Tombs are much more likely to attract tourist dollars, at least from capitalist tourists. Once an embarrassment to town planners, the *hutong* alleys of Beijing are just as much a part of the modern city's heritage as the Forbidden City – perhaps more so, since a visit to them often pays directly into local pockets, instead of government coffers. Pedicab drivers offer tourists trips around the few remaining *hutong* in the city centre, where tourists can gawp at Qing-style buildings, and the sight of people living on the edge of rural poverty, so close to the luxurious apartments of the Party faithful.

The Marco Polo Bridge is still where Marco Polo said it was, although much of what he said *about* it no longer holds true. It is not 'ten miles outside the city', since the metropolis of Beijing has sprawled across every scrap of available land in the place where once there was just an endless tract of marshland waving with reeds and thistles. Nor does the bridge serve its original purpose – not long after being given its new name by the Emperor of Hearty Prosperity, the 'Eternally Pacified' River took the hint and went away for good, leaving the bridge literally high and dry. Although floods and rains and the outflow from a 1950s reservoir may occasionally give it something to span, the bridge usually crosses little more than a shallow dip in the landscape, so overgrown that it looks more like parkland than a river.

A few steps away from the ancient bridge, a sturdy concrete flyover takes care of modern traffic, although the bridge's twentieth century companion is less welcoming to pedestrians. You can still walk across the Marco Polo Bridge, but now it costs you two dollars. There is still a trading post there, but it is a small and sorry open-air 'antiques' market selling bits of fake jade, Chairman Mao lighters, *feng shui* compasses and doubtful fossils. Always, *always* there are the Republican era silver dollars – big round coins like Jubilee Crowns, bearing the fat, bald head of Yuan Shikai and smearings of dirt for that extra touch of authenticity. There were over 184 million minted, and all appear to be still in circulation, all boldly proclaiming that they are worth one dollar, all retailing for twenty and up.

The Great Wall remains the most powerful of symbols – its image is the first that any China visitor sees, snaking across every tourist visa. Entrepreneurs are redeveloping many more sections now, attempting to revitalise the economy of the mountains north of Beijing by making a visit there about more than just seeing the Wall. Giant billboards exhort tourists to come in the dead of winter, when they can ski in the Great Wall's shadow. The wall has also gained a modern, virtual analogue – the Great *Firewall* of China that blocks access from new forms of Western barbarity: our news, our erotica, our idle gossip. For myself, with Google as an Internet homepage and a browsing habit that swings over to the BBC website several times a day, it can be an surprise to discover that those sites are simply not available to the internet user in Beijing.

The concept of Heritage does hold some sway in Beijing. A Kentucky Fried Chicken franchise was ejected from Beihai Park after local pressure groups called it a capitalist step too far. Similar controversy surrounded the Starbucks in the Forbidden City, which gained a kitsch appeal among tourists before its unceremonious removal in July 2007 – the very silliness of it had a certain charm, akin to finding a Hello Kitty franchise in Westminster Abbey. Despite my arch disapproval, I still feel compelled to use the ATM in the Forbidden City, just so I could say that I had. I took money from a hole in the wall at the Centre of the World, and was charged five dollars for the privilege.

There are mixed feelings all round about the incursion of Western-style consumerism into the Forbidden City. After all, don't we *want* them to be more like us? We want them to buy mobile phones, don't we? We want them to listen to the Beatles. We want them to sign trade agreements and consume along with the rest of us. As green politics rises to the fore, we also would like them not to make the same mistakes as us regarding pollution, demolition and emission, but perhaps it is already too late.

Tradition is a double-edged sword. Chinese tradition crippled women for a thousand years with foot binding; it castrated thousands of pauper boys to allow them to work in the palace; it tortured untold millions. The Forbidden City is no longer forbidden or forbidding – it welcomes visitors with their open wallets. Its brand identity, after all, is kept relatively muted, and it does good business – who are we to stop the Chinese from having a coffee at the Centre of the World, where eunuchs once tried to keep bicycles and eye-glasses away from the sight of the last emperors. The Western world already has its junk food and its corporate beverages, like it has the internal combustion engine and the nuclear power plant – should we begrudge the Chinese their coffees Venti and Grande, in the same way we begrudge them greenhouse gases?

But nor is modernisation a bed of roses. The rush of the modern is what hacked the Chinese coast up into treaty ports. Our desire to make the Chinese in our image is what force-fed them opium, and smashed railway lines through ancient city walls. There are poor in London, too, in Washington, in Paris. Beijing was there before them all.

Afterword
Capitalism in the Capital

I have long had difficulty with the bargaining mentality of the Far East. I am an honest Northern European. Tell me what something costs, and I will pay it or I won't. It offends me to wheel and deal over a price, it feels like I am insulting the vendor by rejecting his offer. This can cause all sorts of trouble in the Far East.

If one really wants to buy something in Beijing, one must first speak Mandarin. This slashes the price by about 50 per cent. But that only puts the buyer on a level playing field with locals – the half-price offer is a mark of respect for bothering to learn Chinese. But then the haggling is expected to continue. One only gets the best deal by feigning complete lack of interest in the product under discussion.

There is a flaw in this little cultural etiquette that the Chinese do not seem to have noticed, that customers may simply be genuinely uninterested in buying what they have to sell.

South of Tiananmen, I find a man festooned with traditional musical instruments – flutes, *pipa*, *erhu* and drums. Realising that this is exactly the sort of thing that my father would appreciate, I excitedly engage the vendor in conversation about them. A crowd of hawkers gathers around us, gasping in the breathless awe that custom demands whenever a white face speaks a single word of Chinese, and excitedly chatting to me not as a customer, but as a friend. I recognise some of these people; only yesterday I was batting them away as they pushed fans and Mao wristwatches at me outside my hotel. Now they have lost all interest in selling me anything – instead they are meeting me, chatting, all thought of trinkets forgotten.

The musical pedlar is in seventh heaven, as I take not one, but three of his working instruments. We argue about the *erhu*, not because I don't want it, but because I am not sure how I am going to get the delicate instrument home in my luggage. All in all, the price comes to hardly anything – a few pence, perhaps. Gleefully, I reach into my wallet for the money.

'No!' he says, in horror. 'No! You've got to haggle!'

Land of Swallows and the Land of Qin

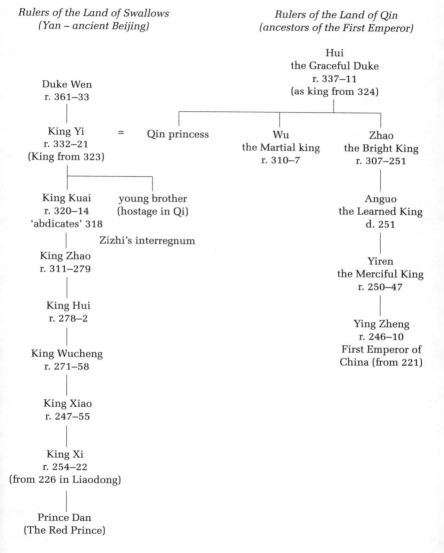

*Rulers of the Land of Swallows
(Yan – ancient Beijing)*

*Rulers of the Land of Qin
(ancestors of the First Emperor)*

Hui
the Graceful Duke
r. 337–11
(as king from 324)

Duke Wen
r. 361–33

King Yi   =   Qin princess
r. 332–21
(King from 323)

Wu
the Martial king
r. 310–7

Zhao
the Bright King
r. 307–251

King Kuai   young brother
r. 320–14   (hostage in Qi)
'abdicates' 318

Anguo
the Learned King
d. 251

Zizhi's interregnum

King Zhao
r. 311–279

Yiren
the Merciful King
r. 250–47

King Hui
r. 278–2

Ying Zheng
r. 246–10
First Emperor of
China (from 221)

King Wucheng
r. 271–58

King Xiao
r. 247–55

King Xi
r. 254–22
(from 226 in Liaodong)

Prince Dan
(The Red Prince)

The Manchu (Qing) Dynasty

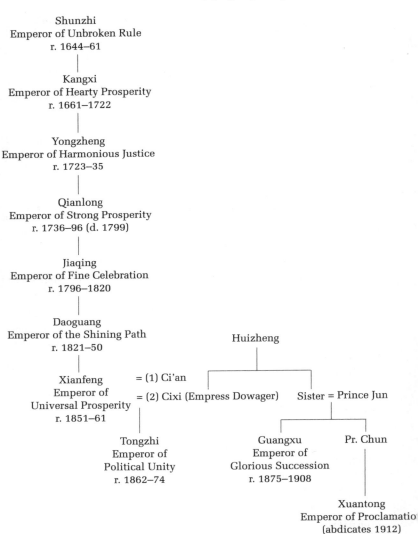

Shunzhi
Emperor of Unbroken Rule
r. 1644–61

Kangxi
Emperor of Hearty Prosperity
r. 1661–1722

Yongzheng
Emperor of Harmonious Justice
r. 1723–35

Qianlong
Emperor of Strong Prosperity
r. 1736–96 (d. 1799)

Jiaqing
Emperor of Fine Celebration
r. 1796–1820

Daoguang
Emperor of the Shining Path
r. 1821–50

Huizheng

Xianfeng   = (1) Ci'an
Emperor of   = (2) Cixi (Empress Dowager)   Sister = Prince Jun
Universal Prosperity
r. 1851–61

Tongzhi   Guangxu   Pr. Chun
Emperor of   Emperor of
Political Unity   Glorious Succession
r. 1862–74   r. 1875–1908

Xuantong
Emperor of Proclamatio
(abdicates 1912)
'The Last Emperor'

Notes

INTRODUCTION
1   Arlington and Lewisohn, *In Search of Old Peking*, page i.

CHAPTER ONE
1   For the age statistics, Barnes, *Rise of Civilization in East Asia*, p. 44. See for example, Derek Bickerton's *Language and Human Behaviour*: 'At a place called Zhoukoudian in northern China, a series of limestone caverns was inhabited by hominids between roughly 500,000 and 200,000 years ago – that is, for about three hundred thousand years, sixty times the entire length of recorded human history. . . Yet during that entire period, not a single structural improvement was made to those caves; the tiny handful of artefacts produced by its inhabitants underwent no change or improvement; "the people of the caves of Zhoukoudian, crouched over their smoky fires, eating their half-cooked bats (Wills 1993:69) without the slightest trace of . . . long-continued elaboration and complexification of the culture".'

2   *Liji* VII, I, 8. Müller/Legge, *Sacred Books of China*, vol. III, p. 369. See also Clements, *Confucius: A Biography*, p. 65.

3   Huangdi – his name is often translated elsewhere as Yellow Emperor, although I assert that China's first true emperor was the man who called himself 'the First

Emperor'. See Clements, *First Emperor of China*, pp. 174–5.

4   Haw, *Beijing: A Concise History*, p. 19.

5   Aldrich, *The Search for a Vanishing Beijing*, p. 35, prefers 'reeds' rather than 'thistles' as a translation of Ji.

6   Crump, *Chan-kuo T'se*, p. 466.

7   Crump, *Chan-kuo T'se*, p. 467–8.

8   Crump, *Chan-kuo T'se*, p. 496. At roughly the same period, far to the south in Chu, Land of the Immaculate, minister Chunshen was drawing a similar analogy, comparing the petty kingdoms to fighting tigers about to exhaust each other, unaware that the slow dog of Qin would pick over their remains. See Clements, *First Emperor of China*, p. 66.

9   Nienhauser, *Grand Scribe's Records*, p. 258; Knoblock and Riegel, *Annals of Lü Buwei*, p. 719.

10   Greater detail can be found in Clements, *The First Emperor of China*, pp. 1–12.

CHAPTER TWO

1   Hinsch, *Women in Early Imperial China*, pp. 46–7. Hinsch regards the case as proof of polyandry, although it is my suspicion that the language of the case obscured a much less official arrangement, and that the three 'husbands' were more likely to have been what modern parlance might call 'deadbeat dads'.

2   Haw, *Beijing: A Concise History*, p. 27.

3   *Ballad of Mulan*, verse three. My translation. The Chinese text is available online at: http://www.yellowbridge.com/onlinelit/mulan.html

4   Ibid., verse ten. Some Chinese believe that Mulan's story dates from slightly later in Chinese history, and claim that she was a warrior in the civil unrest that saw

the establishment of the short-lived Sui dynasty, flourishing in the early seventh century, and that the 'Khan' was actually the future Sui emperor Yangdi, who asked her in vain to be his concubine. But even if this supposition is true, it only serves to highlight just how confused Chinese national identity was at the time – the Sui rulers and their Tang successors were often haunted by their 'barbarian' blood. See, for example, Clements, *Wu*, pp. 23–5.

5   For a more detailed treatment of Taizong's Korean campaign see Clements, *Wu*, pp. 30–5.

6   Werner, *A Dictionary of Chinese Mythology*, pp. 247–9.

7   Meyer, *Peking as a Sacred City*, p. 56.

8   Birrell, *Chinese Mythology*, pp. 165–7; for the specific Beijing associations, see Bodde (ed.), *Annual Customs and Festivals in Peking*, p. 59. The custom of wearing a magpie bridge insignia on the seventh day of the seventh lunar month would continue through the century of the Yuan dynasty, when one might also expect a sense of a lost Chinese culture to pervade. It largely died out with the arrival of the Ming dynasty.

9   Jin, *Beijing Legends*, p. 84.

CHAPTER THREE

1   Yule, *Marco Polo*, p. 331.

2   Yule, *Marco Polo*, p. 375.

3   Yule, *Marco Polo*, pp. 364–5.

4   Yule, *Marco Polo*, p. 367.

5   Aldrich, *Search for a Vanishing Beijing*, p. 133.

6   Haw, *Marco Polo's China*, p. 115.

7   Yule, *Marco Polo* II, p. 9.

8   Haw, *Marco Polo's China*, pp. 78–9.

9   Yule, *Marco Polo* II, p. 3; Haw, *Marco Polo's China*, p. 95 and p. 190.

10 Yule, *Marco Polo* II, p. 4.

11 Jin, *Beijing Legends*, pp. 56–8. The story is suspiciously similar to a legend from over the border in Korea, where part of the casting process for the 8th century Divine Bell of King Seongdeok reputedly included the sacrifice of the lead artisan's daughter.

CHAPTER FOUR

1   Haw, *Beijing: A Concise History*, p. 53. For reasons of space and simplicity, I have referred to other cities by their most common modern name and not the many permutations of their own histories.

2   Note that some Chinese sources suggest that the Prince of Yan enjoyed supernatural assistance even in his days as a prince, and that before he even made his bid for the emperorship, he enjoyed Daoist advice concerning the renovation of Beijing. See Meyer, *Peking as a Sacred City*, p. 147; Arlington and Lewisohn, *In Search of Old Peking*, p. 28.

3   Jin, *Beijing Legends*, p. 10.

4   For a detailed list matching city feature to body parts, see Arlington and Lewisohn, *In Search of Old Peking*, pp. 338–9. Because somebody always asks: Nezha's penis is thought to be represented by the bridge that dangles south from the Rear Gate.

5   Jin, *Beijing Legends*, p. 52. If a *tael* is an ounce of silver, then the 4.8 million found at the Ten Vaults site would be worth roughly £35 million at 2007 prices.

6   *Analects*: Book II, chapter 1. See Clements, *Confucius*, p. 67.

7   Jin, *Beijing Legends*, pp. 39–40.

8   Jin, *Beijing Legends*, pp. 43–4. Jin fails to explain just what the emperor required in the building, but the way he recounts the builders' excitement at the cage design implies that they had been given some sort of mathematical-architectural puzzle to solve.

9   Shang, *Tales of Empresses and Imperial Consorts in China*, pp. 281–4.

10   Aldrich, *Vanishing Beijing*, p. 366. Today, the Eight Sights are loaded with poetic associations, but most of them come from long after the Ming dynasty, as later emperors and poets have concocted verses to retroactively justify their selection. A leading contributor was the Qianlong Emperor, who dutifully dashed off poems about several of the sites, and then had them carved into stone monuments to remind people just how impressive they were. He is also responsible for a name-change; the 'Golden Terrace' was originally called the Miao Family Estate, but Qianlong was worried about the implications of associating something so famous with a single clan, and came up with something vaguer.

CHAPTER FIVE

1   Wakeman, *Great Enterprise*, p. 581.

2   Clements, *Pirate King*, pp. 160–1.

3   Qianlong Emperor, quoted in Haw, *Beijing: A Concise History*, p. 79.

4   Macartney, *An Embassy to China*, pp. 105–6.

5   We should, perhaps, observe that something similar happened in many other cities. I am writing these words in my London flat, itself comprising the servants' quarters of a middle-class nineteenth-century residence.

6   Gordon, quoted in Broudehoux, *The Making and Selling of Post-Mao Beijing*, p. 58.

7   McGhee, quoted in Broudehoux, *The Making and Selling of Post-Mao Beijing*, p. 59.

8   As if matters were not confusing enough, a version of the old Wade-Giles system endures on Taiwan (the *Republic* of China), which refuses to use a Communist invention. However, the Republican government in exile on Taiwan still clings to the notion that Nanjing should be the capital back on the mainland, and consequently refers to Beijing as Beiping (in Wade-Giles, Peip'ing), or Northern Peace.

CHAPTER SIX

1   Aldrich, *Search for a Vanishing Beijing*, p. 61.

2   Clements, *Mao*, p. 95.

CHAPTER SEVEN

1   See, for example, the anonymous article 'Going Underground', from the *China Daily*.

2   Clements, *Mao*, p. 135.

3   *China Daily*, quoted in Broudehoux, *The Making and Selling of post-Mao Beijing*, p. 152.

CHAPTER EIGHT

1   Broudehoux, *The Making and Selling of Post-Mao Beijing*, p. 154.

2   Yardley, J., 'No Spitting on the Road to Olympic Glory'.

3   The condition of Chinese toilets has become a pet subject for my wife, who is quite happy to defecate in a bucket in the forest in her native Finland, but has paroxysms of anguish about Chinese facilities. She

eventually began keeping careful accounts of available options, and reports that she has found the 'Best Toilet in China'. At the risk of causing a ruinous rush of thrill-seekers, it is at the Temple of Confucius in Xi'an.

4   Beijing Olympics press release, 10 March 2007. http://en.beijing2008.cn/70/44/article214024470.shtml

5   'A New Wave of Oppression Justified by the Olympics', http://www.rsf.org/article.php3?id_article=2287

6   Broudehoux, *The Making and Selling of Post-Mao Beijing*, pp. 199–20.

7   I am not alone in finding the hawkers of Simatai to be 'the most relentless and irritating'. See Harper, *Beijing*, p. 148.

8   Broudehoux, *The Making and Selling of Post-Mao Beijing*, p. 66. The 'Hong Kong' replica is actually halfway between the old colony and Canton, but the point still stands. Hong Kong has the 'theme park' mentality, while Beijing clings to historical provenance.

9   Broudehoux, *The Making and Selling of Post-Mao Beijing*, p. 84.

Bibliography

Aldrich, M. *The Search for a Vanishing Beijing: A Guide to China's Capital Through the Ages*. Hong Kong: Hong Kong University Press, 2006.

Anon. 'Going Underground', *China Daily*, 30 December 2005, p. 10.

Anon. 'Ancient Human Unearthed in China', 2 April 2007, BBC.co.uk.

Anon. 'Games "catalyst for China abuses"', 29 April 2007, BBC.co.uk.

Anon. 'Forbidden City Starbucks Closes', 14 July 2007, BBC.co.uk.

Arlington, L, and William Lewisohn. *In Search of Old Peking*. Hong Kong: Kelly and Walsh, 1935 [repr. 1967].

Barnes, G. *The Rise of Civilization in East Asia: The Archaeology of China, Korea and Japan*. London, Thames & Hudson, 1999.

Beijing Astronomy Society. *Zhongguo Gudai Tianwenxue Chengjiu [Achievements in Ancient Chinese Astronomy]*. Beijing: Kexue Jishu Chubanshe [Science and Technology Press], 1987.

Bickerton, D. *Language and Human Behaviour*. London, UCL Press, 1996.

Birrell, A. *Chinese Mythology: An Introduction*. Baltimore: The Johns Hopkins University Press, 1993.

Bodde, D. *Annual Customs and Festivals in Peking as recorded in the Yen-ching Sui-shih-chi by Tun Li-Ch'en*. Peiping (Beijing): Henri Vetch, 1936.

Bredon, J. *Peking: A Historical and Intimate Description of its Chief Places of Interest*. Shanghai: Kelly & Walsh, 1920.

Broudehoux, A. *The Making and Selling of Post-Mao Beijing*. New York: Routledge, 2004.

Clements, J. *Confucius: A Biography*. Stroud: Sutton Publishing, 2004.

——. *Pirate King: Coxinga and the Fall of the Ming Dynasty*. Stroud: Sutton Publishing, 2004.

——. *The First Emperor of China*. Stroud: Sutton Publishing, 2006.

——. *Mao*. London: Haus Publishing, 2006.

——. *Wu: The Chinese Empress Who Schemed, Seduced and Murdered Her Way to Become a Living God*. Stroud: Sutton Publishing, 2007.

Crump, J. *Chan-kuo Ts'e*. Ann Arbor: Center for Chinese Studies, University of Michigan, 1996.

Gao, X. *The World Cultural Heritage in Beijing: Peking Man Site at Zhoukoudian*. Beijing: Beijing Meishu Sheying Chubanshe (Beijing Fine Arts Pictorial Publisher), 2004.

Gray, J. *Rebellions and Revolutions: China from the 1800s to the 1980s*. Oxford: Oxford University Press, 1990.

Elder, C. (ed.) *Old Peking: City of the Ruler of the World*. Hong Kong: Oxford University Press, 1997.

'Fei-Shi'. *Guide to Peking and Its Environs*. Tianjin: The Tientsin Press, 1909.

Harper, D. *Beijing*. Melbourne: Lonely Planet Publications, 2002.

Haw, S. *Marco Polo's China: A Venetian in the realm of Khubilai Khan.* London: Routledge, 2006.

——. *Beijing: A Concise History.* London: Routledge, 2007.

Hinsch, B. *Women in Early Imperial China.* Lanham, Maryland: Rowman & Littlefield, 2002.

Jenner, D. *Letters from Peking.* London: Oxford University Press, 1967.

Jin, S. *Beijing Legends.* Beijing: Panda Books, 1982.

Jones, K. and Anthony Pan. *Culture Shock! Beijing.* London: Kuperard, 2003.

Knoblock, J. and Jeffrey Riegel (eds). *The Annals of Lü Buwei.* Stanford: Stanford University Press, 2000.

Macartney, G. *An Embassy to China, being the journal kept by Lord Macartney during his Embassyy to the Emperor Ch'ien-lung 1793–1794.* London: Folio Society, 2004.

Meyer, J. *Peking as a Sacred City.* Taipei: Orient Cultural Service Asian Folklore and Social Life Monographs, 1976.

——. *The Dragons of Tiananmen: Beijing as a Sacred City.* Columbia, SC: University of South Carolina Press, 1991 [revised edition of Meyer, 1976].

Naquin, S. *Peking: Temples and City Life, 1400–1900.* Berkeley: University of California Press, 2000.

Nienhauser, W. *The Grand Scribe's Records: Volume VII, The Memoirs of Pre-Han China.* Bloomington: Indiana University Press, 1994.

Paludan, A. *Chronicle of the Chinese Emperors: The Reign-by-Reign Record of the Rulers of Imperial China.* London: Thames & Hudson, 1998.

Schiffer, J. *The Legendary Creatures of the Shan Hai Ching.* Taipei, Hwa Kang Press, 1978.

Shang, X. *Tales of Empresses and Imperial Consorts in China*. Hong Kong: Hai Feng Publishing, 1994.

Sit, V. *Beijing: The Nature and Planning of a Chinese Capital City*. Chichester: John Wiley and Sons, 1995.

Shapiro, H. *Peking Man*. London: Allen & Unwin, 1975.

Tarpy, C. 'Jewels in the Ash: China's Extraordinary Fossil Site', in *National Geographic*, August 2005, pp. 86–97.

Tsai, H. *Perpetual Happiness: the Ming Emperor Yongle*. Seattle: University of Washington Press, 2001.

Wakeman, F. *The Great Enterprise: The Manchu Reconstruction of Imperial Order in Seventeenth-Century China*. Berkeley: University of California Press, 1985.

Waley-Cohen, F. *The Sextants of Beijing: Global Currents in Chinese History*. New York: W.W. Norton and Company, 1999.

Werner, E. *A Dictionary of Chinese Mythology*. New York: Julian Press, 1969.

Wood, F. *Hand-Grenade Practice in Peking*. London: John Murray, 2000.

Xu, C. *Old Beijing: People, Houses and Lifestyles*. Beijing: Foreign Languages Press, 2001.

Yardley, J. 'No Spitting on the Road to Olympic Glory', *New York Times*, 17 April 2007.

Yule, H. (ed) *The Book of Ser Marco Polo The Venetian, Concerning the Kingdoms and Marvels of the East*. 2 vols. London: John Murray, 1871.

Index